Politically incorrect and bourgeois: Nariva Swamp is sufficient onto itself

Cheryl Lans

"But what is your price for the land? " asked Pakhom.
"Our price," answered the Starshina, "is only 1000 roubles per day."
Pakhom did not understand this day-rate at all.
"How many dessiatins (2.8 acres) would that include?" he inquired presently.
"We do not reckon in that way," said the Starshina. "We sell only by the day. That is to say, as much land as you can walk round in a day, that much land is yours." (Leo Tolstoy, How Much Land Does a Man Require?)

Table of contents

List of acronyms

SEAGA	Socioeconomic and Gender Analysis (FAO)
FAO	Food and Agriculture Organisation
EMA	Environmental Management Authority
CFCA	Caribbean Forest Conservation Association
IMA	Institute of Marine Affairs
ISLE	Island Sustainability, Livelihood and Equity Programme
MALMR	Ministry of Agriculture, Land and Marine Resources
UWI	University of the West Indies
CAREC	Caribbean Epidemiology Centre
GORTT	Government of the Republic of Trinidad and Tobago
PRA	Participatory Rural Appraisal
NEDECO	Netherlands Engineering Consultants
TRVL	Trinidad Regional Virus Lab
O.C.T.A	Overseas Technical Co-operation Agency
EIA	Environmental Impact Assessment
CIAT	Centre Internacional de Agricultura Tropical
JICA	Japanese International Corporation Agency
NFM	National Flour Mills
GEF	Global Environment Facility
WLCC	National Wetlands Committee

Preface

Writers typically state that their work reflects their own opinions and not of their employers or collaborators and this is explicitly true for this book. The book is in two parts. The first part is a reflection of my own thoughts on the Nariva Swamp issue which cannot be stated publicly in Trinidad without economic and social consequences. The second part is a modified version of a report prepared for the Centre for Gender and Development at the University of the West Indies, St Augustine, Trinidad and this is where the first sentence becomes necessary.

Cover photo: USDA Image Number: 01di1466

Pages: 161   ISBN 978-0-9783468-0-5
Printed by lulu.com

Introduction

In the decade since I conducted research on the Nariva Swamp I have not changed my mind about the outcome that I would have liked to see: that Nariva Swamp should be accepted as sufficient onto itself with its own right to exist untampered with ---which does not mean that it has untrammelled rights to expand beyond its current boundaries. I was involved in two research projects in the Swamp because the new co-management discourse seemed to limit "stakeholders" to those physically present; so I was there once or twice a week setting up an ecotourism venture that was as close to my desired outcome as I could get (with CNIRD, Amar Wahab and Prof. Peter Bacon) and conducting a gender-based analysis on governance aspects of the Nariva Swamp. I also paid one of the ecotourism participants to collect data on medicinal plants for my thesis. Indeed I am listed as an "external user" in Kacal (2000).

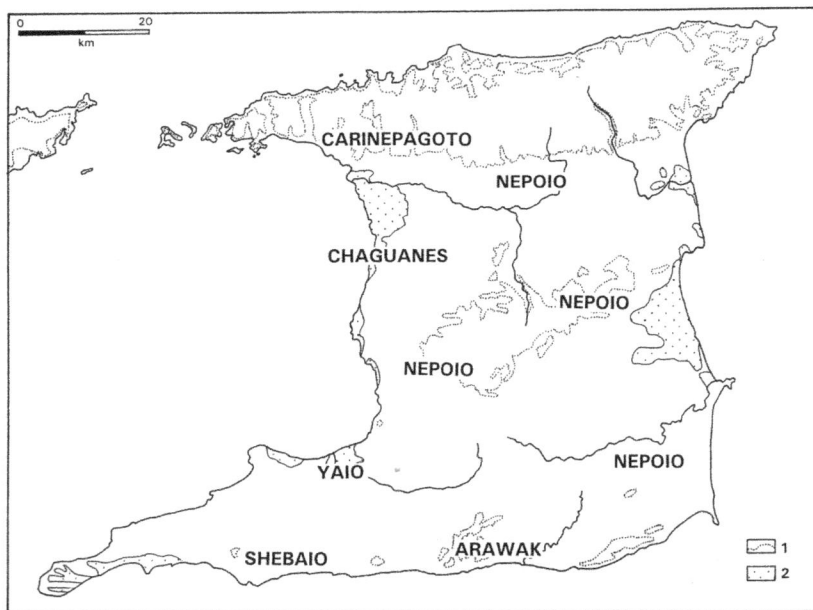

Legend: (1) 100-m contourline; (2) swamps and marshes. Source: Boomert, 2006.

Fig 1. Map of Trinidad showing the major swamps and Amerindian groups ca. 1600

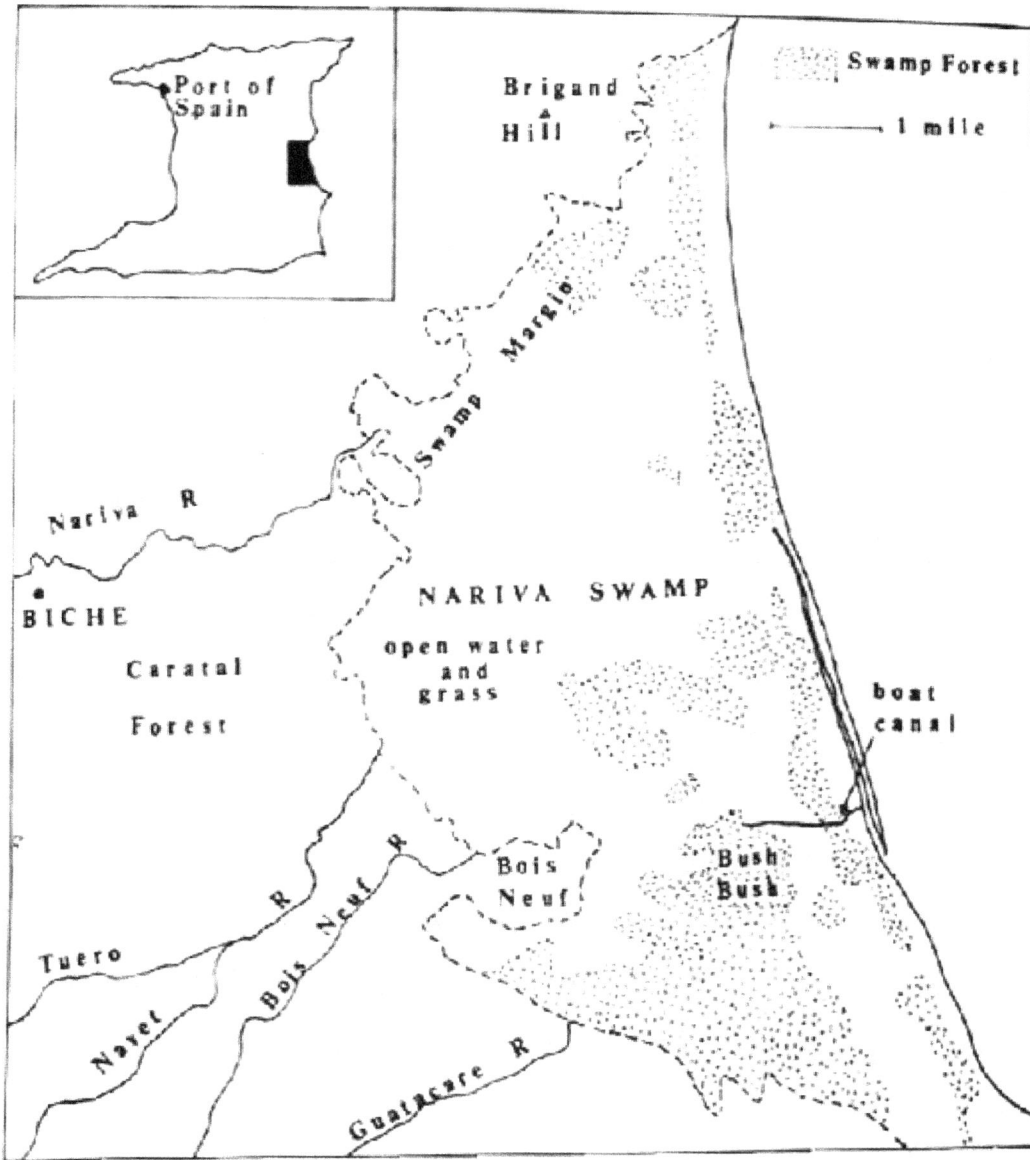

Fig 2. The location of Nariva Swamp in Trinidad also showing the major rivers (source Aitken, 1973)

In recent years haven't more new species been found in "untouched nature" than in "wise use nature"? Doesn't the occasional jaunt into "unused nature" by scientists and lay public alike have tremendous value? This view is personal of course reflecting my orientation as concerned about the environment and in finding that untouched Nature has immense value for exploration and discovery, plus my disappointment with some of the supposed naturalness and beauty of existing sites.

I remember my sister "playing with words" saying she would have to be a "mad-damn-ass" to go back to one particular place in north Trinidad; and as a child she had not spent one-third of the time in the "pristine" forest as my brother and I. Blue basin was also a disappointment. In hikes with the Field Naturalists there was always the sense that the experience "could have been better" if the site was "pristine." In the last five years with the use of on-location video cameras hooked to the Internet and helicopters to track wildlife hunts (most animals ignore them or don't notice them), scientists and naturalists have realized that many of their previous knowledge claims were inaccurate. These new scientific tools are another reason to have "pristine" wilderness in place for study; especially since some of the previous inaccurate data has been used by sociobiologists to make false claims about people in general and women in particular.

Political ecologists have tended to favour solutions that come from the local community; however the push for co-management of the Swamp and even the call for ecotourism came from outside the Swamp. For a national resource like the Swamp there has to be more consideration of who is a member of the concerned community, how strongly to link rights to place, and whose rights are affected by any plans and strategies. Not all communities are coherent, united, or strongly attached to place (Clapp, 2004). If longevity in place were at the root of being 'local', then the strongest ethical claims to the landscape would belong to the many species that constitute the swamp ecosystem. Tompkins et al. (2002) claim that participatory approaches cannot in themselves produce sustainable utilisation of resources. They write that there are limits to co- management based on the complexity of the resource, the size of the user pool, the reality of the social construction of networks and spaces in which co-management takes place and the geographical area.

In June 2000, 23 Kernahan residents who paid the surveying and legal fees obtained a 30 year lease on 3.5 acre blocks of land in Block E under the Ministry of Agriculture's Accelerated Land Distribution Programme for which they were to pay $90/rent a year (Doodhai, 2000). The government could have used the whole Nariva swamp controversy to remove all of the squatters who at the time had no infrastructure (roads, electricity, water) in a move towards a society in which all are required to obey the law.

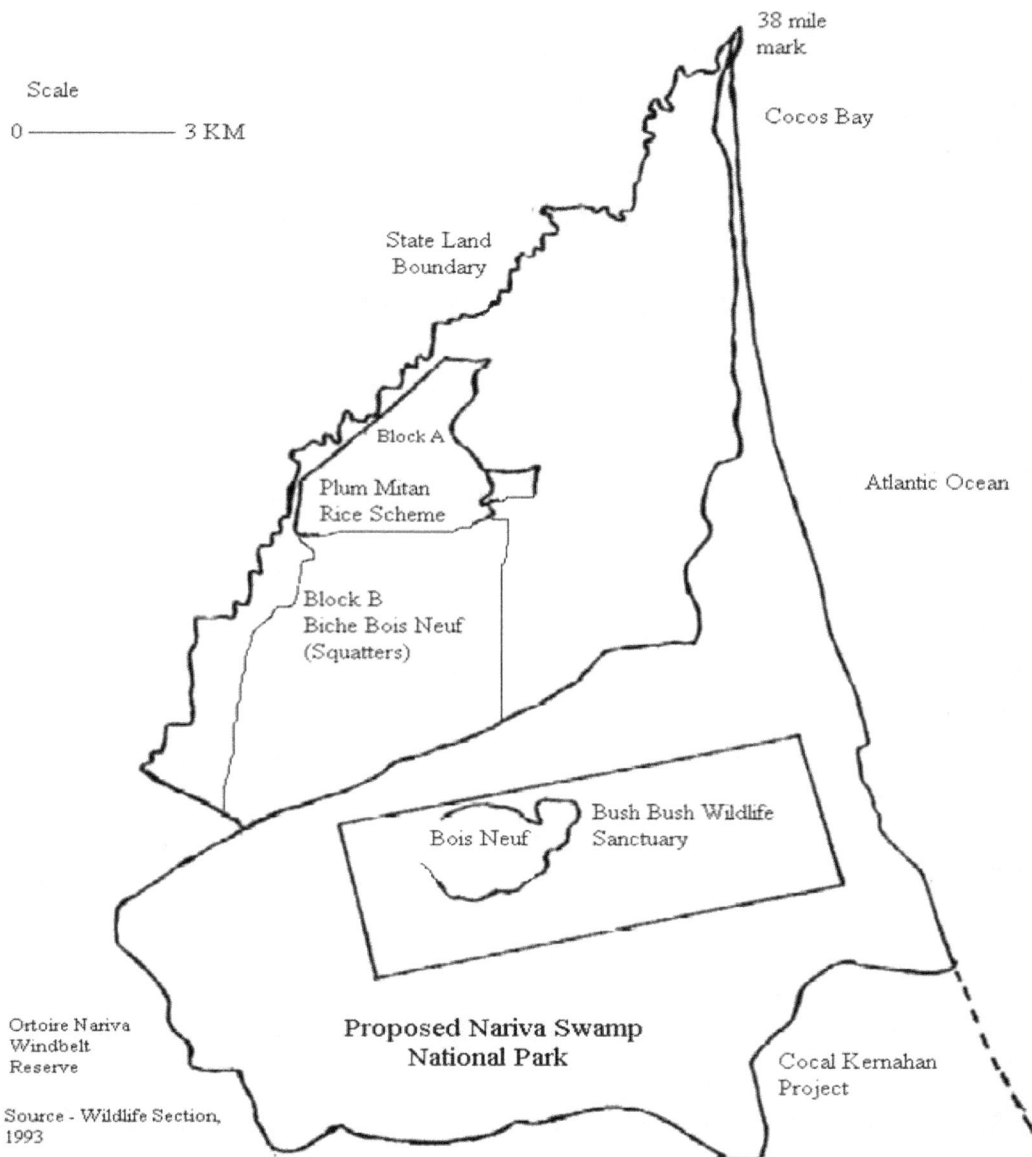

Scale

0 —————— 3 KM

38 mile mark

Cocos Bay

State Land Boundary

Atlantic Ocean

Block A

Plum Mitan Rice Scheme

Block B Biche Bois Neuf (Squatters)

Bois Neuf

Bush Bush Wildlife Sanctuary

Proposed Nariva Swamp National Park

Ortoire Nariva Windbelt Reserve

Cocal Kernahan Project

Source - Wildlife Section, 1993

Fig 3. Location of major sectors in the Nariva Swamp (source Wildlife Section, 1993)

Small-scale squatters had not been in the Swamp before 1930 (Sletto community map from 1997) and older inhabitants were at a stage of life when retiring to a more developed community with schools, health facilities and public transport would have been desirable. Sletto (2002) claims that 20 of the 61 village households in Kernahan were established during the 1970s in an affort to create a "new Penal." Sletto's other publications do not differ significantly from the 2002 work in their data.

When the Nariva conflict was at its height, the dissolution of Caroni Ltd and distribution of its lands was being seriously talked about and at least one of the large farmers was allowed to farm on Caroni lands after the EIA was completed. I doubt that anyone in the country would have objected if the small farmers were allowed to lease lands there as well. Instead government officials probably did not want to be bested by a "bunch of environmentalists" and chose to follow the tradition of "regularizing" those who had already "taken all the land that they required." Kalema-Zikusoka (2005) points out that it is the "problem" wildlife that reduce the value of the surrounding land which then attracts poor people and squatters to that particular area which has no competing human users. Driver (2001) quotes reports stating that it is the avoidance of crop theft that drives squatters to steep inaccessible hillsides; it is not that these areas (the Swamp or the hills) themselves had any socio-cultural value to the people living there.

In essence my argument is that the whole island does not need to be developed. If the eastern side remains undeveloped that would allow the animal populations space to regenerate. Asa Wright alone cannot provide that space, especially for what Bacon (1988) identified as rare species such as bivalves (*Anodontites leotaudi*, *Mycetopoda siliquosa* and *Mytilopsis domingenesis*), water snakes (*Helicops angulatus*, *Eunectes murinus gigas*), the manatee (*Trichesus manatus*) and otters (*Lutra enudris*). Conservation and preservation approaches are no longer commonly accepted and have been criticized by Siurua (2006) as "fortress conservation."

 Siurua prefers community conservation models based on the recognition that "communities down the millennia have developed elaborate rituals and practices to limit offtake levels, restrict access to critical resources, and distribute harvests" but then acknowledges that community-based options are no "magic solution." Siurua also acknowledges that certain species (tigers and rhinos are the examples used and could be considered equivalent to Nariva's snakes and "alligators") cannot be co-managed. Sylvia Kacal (1997) stated at the Nariva Swamp Seminar in May 1996 "it is clear that small island states cannot set aside many large wilderness areas for strict preservation." Clear to whom? Who has ever said that it is clear that small islands cannot set aside large areas like Point Lisas, or La Brea for industrial development? If an island is not too small for industrial estates how can it be too small for National Parks?

Kernahan and Cascadoux communities use birds, cascadura, conch, snakes, agouti, caiman and crabs from the swamp. The Wildlife Section (1993) documented that they illegally sold birds to make a living and in fact some species like the blue and gold macaws (*Ara ararauna*) were wiped out by the pet trade and the *Ara manilata* (red-bellied macaw) was threatened due to habitat destruction of the palm (*Roystonea oleracea*) (Wildlife Section, 1993).

Community members told researchers that their survival was more important than that of the snakes and alligators that threatened them. Their livelihood also took precedence over having a balanced environment and one farmer had cut as much as 35 acres of land for cultivation (Cross et al., 1999). There are many, many examples of non-environmental attitudes in the Masters thesis of Amar Wahab and in his 1997 publication on "The Status of Women in the Nariva Wetland Communities" and in Durbal (2000). However I do not want to quote extensively from the work of my colleagues because they may not share my opinions. Where are the fairy tales of the manatee as the local equivalent of mermaids - are they not in fact treated "as a cook up"? Here lies the flaw in the majority of the work done by external researchers on community management. These researchers applied studies from other societies on the Trinidad situation without checking to see if Trinidad and Tobago inhabitants had similar attitudes and behaviours. The one exception is the work of Sletto (2002) who did not have a co-management agenda and saw accurately the social construction of the "noble swmp dweller." The other researchers did not even acknowledge that Trinbagonians do not have the "live to work" attitude necessary for survival in countries like the USA. The local work attitudes would affect the cost and viability of any community based project.

Someone once said that Trinidadians divide animals into two categories those that bite and those that "bite nice" (are good to eat). Is it true? There have been no studies on the matter. But there was a case in which a hand-raised owl with no fear of humans landed on a north coast beach and was summarily killed. Shouldn't an attitudinal study have preceded any discussion of ecosystem co-management? Mahy (1997) for example quotes in her thesis that traditional forest users are more likely than other groups to employ sustainable techniques because they know the resource that they are using and are unlikely to deplete the resources and move to another location. Worth (1967) found that local hunters in the Nariva Swamp did not know one rat from another (*Zygodontomys brevicauda*, *Oryzomys laticeps* and *Heteromys anomalus*) and had knowledge only of the agoutis and larger game animals. They also did not know that there were two different kinds of murine opossums (*Marmosa* sp.), not just young and adults of different sizes. Depletion and moving (shifting cultivation) has long been the practice in Trinidad, in the swamps, on the mountains, as slash and burn and other such practices (Wildlife Section, 1993). Shifting cultivation was sustainable with smaller populations, but is no longer. Mahy correctly claimed that local communities can cost effectively patrol and police local resources but locally based non-corrupt forestry officials would be more effective still. The community norms that she refers to were not in operation either between the small and large farmers or by the small farmers themselves who claimed to fight over the truck borne water supply (Cross et al., 1999) and do not collaborate in other areas (Hosein and Cross, 2000).

Seemingly rigorously ignored by external researchers on Nariva were the consumption studies by Daniel Miller (1994) which stated clearly how devoted Trinidadians are to modernity, consumption and material objects – a culture seemingly ill suited to co-management. A possible future social study relevant to environmental issues in the Caribbean could entail what Willems-Braun (1997) calls "buried epistemologies." He defines postcoloniality as the condition in which colonial pasts continue to organize experience in the present. Colonialist cultural practices remain endemic as vestigial thinking that permeates everyday life.

The impact of past colonial practices is recognised in the impact that Spanish land laws and early sugarcane planters' behaviour has had on the prevalence of squatting (Driver, 2001). However there are no studies on how vestigial colonial thinking may shape the nature/progress duality that seems to exist in Trinidad as a "buried epistemology" or "bad epistemic habit" that is naturalised as "common sense."

I wonder if these attitudes are also compounded by the practice of transposing Indian and African practices onto the Trinidadian landscape – which is then never fully embraced as having value for being tropical American. For example why are Trinbagonians afraid of owls? Is that something they learnt from the Amerindians

like the superstitions around silk cotton trees; or is it a belief that was brought to the islands approximately 200 years ago?

The colonizing power inherent in particular ways of rendering landscape visible (Willems-Braun, 1997) could be applied to the constant stream of externally-funded reports on the "development" of Nariva Swamp, and the uncritical acceptance of the research conducted by external researchers embedded in the country for a few months. An external researcher can bring new insights into a situation that has become bogged down into settled camps but that depends on his/her perspective and preconceived notions. Kupfer (2003) claims that attitudes and interests sometimes determine the aesthetic appreciation people have of Nature. Noncompetitive individuals may approach a steep slope as exploratory rather than as confrontational, whereas some surfers view every wave as a personal challenge. External researchers in the Nariva case did not approach Trinidad and Tobago as a research situation to explore; they came and confronted preservationists. For example Trinidad-based Driver (2001) claims that "science-policy processes have created and sustained an environmental category: the degraded landscape" ignoring human created landscapes that would not exist without continuous human intervention. Driver does not acknowledge that the most dramatic changes in the Northern Range being described have happened within the lifetimes of the "bourgeois" environmental critics, before their eyes, and that they did not stand at the foothills and exclaim at the state of the Northern Range – they were frequently hiking there and had been for decades. Driver prefers to claim that the landscape has always been humanly shaped and since it is not "pristine"; further changes should therefore be unremarked upon.

Rather than truly bringing into being a Trinidadian perspective Leach and Fairhead brought their African field experience and Anthropology's 21st century "search for a subject" and "atonement for past colonialist sins" into the Trinidadian context. African field experience is just that "African"; the Caribbean has more perspectives and histories than African ones and we don't have any African game animals or much African-origin flora and fauna although *Aedes aegypti* is said to have come to Trinidad during the slave trade (Woods, 1967). Would researchers bring British experience to a Canadian field study and claim immediate expertise and relevance? Probably not – but they would be more correct than in the former instance. There are many cultural differences and complex historical and sociological factors in the Caribbean. The state of the environment in Haiti and the Dominican Republic for example may be attributed to the excessive price that Haiti had to pay to France for independence. But there may be other factors that have resulted in a green Dominican Republic versus an over-harvested Haiti. It seems that colonial attitudes are still present in Anthropology but its practitioners seem to have found a more acceptable target than "natives" in "aspiring to middle class professionals."

Mahy correctly identifies the co-management of the marine turtles on the Matura beach on the north-coast of Trinidad as a successful example. However in the Matura case there was no other alternative and the species in question, leatherback turtles, was not continuously present but visiting the island for a specific reproductive period. In the Nariva Swamp there was an alternative. One successful ecotourism project

13

does not mean that everything else should be co-managed; a mix of options would be the best approach – each matched appropriately to difference scenarios. A national park with a constant stream of visitors would have provided the jobs the community needed and encouraged the protection of the wildlife.

This does not necessitate swamp-based inhabitants; they could have commuted from legally owned lands in nearby Manzanilla. In this book I make the opposite argument to the Kernahan inhabitants. Given the fact that many have land and property elsewhere and like the majority of Trinbagonians have no history and/or culture of harmonious environmental existence, the ecological integrity of the swamp is therefore of more importance than and incompatible with the location of "poor squatters" there. For example Worth (1967) naively describes the "progressive decline" of the Bush Bush rodents after he started to trap them and amputate their toes in order to identify them; not acknowledging that his human presence and interference may have contributed to their decline. He writes that he "fails to weep" for them and he moves on to trap birds that are banded rather than mutilated.

Brydon (2006) wonders if anthropology should abandon nature altogether rather than move from a search for the Noble Savage, to the myth that natives have always lived more harmoniously with nature than non-natives (even in the face of empirical studies of disharmony, error, and ecological destruction). Suppose social science policies like "wise use" were just social scientists looking after their own jobs? After all "unused nature" is hardly something for them to study; especially since very few studies of any kind have been done on freshwater wetlands (Bacon, 1998). But co-management entails the setting up and maintenance of community organizations, the constant need to foster community empowerment, to facilitate (Sylvia Kacal, 2000) and negotiate and the on-going nature and on-going funding of such an enterprise – in fact a long-term job(I am not suggesting that environmentally-based job creation is wrong – just pointing out possible underlying motives).

For example Keeler and Pemberton (1996) claim that "one of the positive features of this situation [conflict in Nariva Swamp] in that both local and international environmental groups are firmly behind the idea of sustainable use by Nariva by people, including its use for agriculture. There is very little sentiment or rhetoric for simply making Nariva into a park or denying all uses except ecotourism. This attitude makes sustainable consensus solutions more feasible."
Keeler and Pemberton were co-creators of an interdisciplinary research team of UWI

and University of Georgia scientists established to conduct research on the sustainable development of the Nariva Swamp. Their objectives were to promote wise use of the Ramsar site, to improve the welfare of the Kernahan community and the wider society from the use of Nariva's resources and to contribute to UWI teaching and research. The sub components were (1) Social Assessment and Conservation Management of Nariva Swamp (2) The Contribution of Nutrition to Sustainable Development of the Nariva Swamp (3) Hydrology and Water Management (4) Soil Properties and Implications for Sustainable Management (5) The Development of a Nariva Swamp National Park as an Eco-Tourism Site (6) Sustainable use and commercialisation of wetland resource organisms. Basically the project called for economic development that would have required a lot of professional management expertise for its continuance – professional job creation.

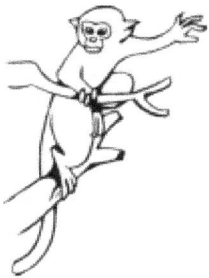 Left out of this project, the Centre for Gender and Development Studies obtained funding from CIDA and other sources and conducted gender sensitive research project in the swamp. The research was conducted in collaboration with the Island, Sustainability, Livelihood and Equity Programme (ISLE). ISLE was in turn a collaborative project of the University of the Philippines, Hasanuddin University in Indonesia, Dalhousie University, Nova Scotia Agricultural College, UWI and the Technical University of Nova Scotia. The Nariva human community was studied by young participant researchers (Cross et al., 1999; Durbal, 2000; Hosein and Cross, 2000). They used interviews, participant observation, ethnography and participatory approaches that included workshops on time lines, resource use charts and community and benefit flow charts. The governance aspect was to look at governance and social control at various levels (micro, macro), history of policy, how and why policies changed over time, impact of international policy community on local decision making and policy formation and a gender analysis of the policy assumptions (the second part of this book).

The ecofeminist approach that best fits this book comes from "Reweaving the World: The Emergence of Ecofeminism (1990) in which the editors, Irene Diamond and Gloria Orenstein lay out three strands in ecofeminism (quoted in Mack-Canty, 2004). One strand emphasizes that social justice has to be achieved in concert with the well-being of the Earth since human life is dependent on the Earth. Another strand in ecofeminism is spiritual, emphasizing that the Earth is sacred unto itself. A third strand emphasizes the necessity of sustainability—a need to learn the many ways we can walk the fine line between using the Earth as a resource while respecting the Earth's needs. MacGregor (2004) writes that a focus on women acting on "survival" or "subsistence" imperatives erases moral choice and practices of making principled decisions to act, or not to act, in particular ways by focussing solely on "the view from below": the moral insight that comes out of so-called unmediated experiences of survival. MacGregor (2004) states the problems that arise from the lack of acknowledgement that many of the women who ecofeminists romanticize as exhibiting a "subsistence perspective" or "barefoot epistemology" do so in conditions that they did not choose and that "lifestyle" does not necessarily determine human morality.

Other writers (Huggan, 2004; Driver. 2001) seem to mock moral arguments, ignoring the reality that both Christian and non-Christian populations use moral reasoning. Driver therefore cannot identify with the bourgeois "sarcastic "editorial writer who wants to stop following the law and squat on state land to avoid land taxes and other nuisances. Jacques (2006) claims that the environmental skeptic Peter Huber argues that humans have no moral obligation to non-human nature because humanity has the ability to dominate and control nature and this is what Judeo-Christian doctrine dictates (deep anthropocentrism - enlightened anthropocentrism favours saving coral reefs for future medical benefits or for biodiversity reasons and for resources that humans use currently and that may be used for future generations). Even the law in most former British colonies (and probably other countries) is based on Judeo-Christian religion, so how can morality be dismissed as a non-issue? Many of the laws on the books in Trinidad and Tobago have not been changed since their creation under the British colonial system (Tompkins et al., 2002). Huggan and Driver don't seem to realize that it is in fact Nature that is the non moral agent.

Siurua (2006) discusses how David Schmidtz divides morality into two parts: a "morality of personal aspiration," encompassing the ethical convictions and ideals according to which a person orients his or her actions, and a "morality of interpersonal constraint," which forms the basis of institutional arrangements to regulate social interactions between individuals pursuing their personal goals. Schmidtz argues that strict preservationism (in the sense of a rejection of any instrumental utilization of nature in protected areas, often motivated by nonanthropocentrism) may be acceptable and justified as part of a morality of the first kind, but as long as the costs of actual preservation are to be borne by people who do not share preservationist values, the promotion of preservationism as the foundation of interpersonal morality is doomed to failure and consequently ought not to be undertaken. I would argue that preservationism ought not to be undertaken with people who do not have preservationist values who as I said at the beginning of the Introduction to this book - should have been relocated to a more comfortable environment at State cost.

The push towards quantifying Nature as 'ecosystem services', or the economic benefits provided by natural ecosystems is part of a market-oriented mechanism for conservation says McCauley (2006) in a much-discussed article in the journal Nature. The underlying assumption is that if scientists can identify ecosystem services, like the Manzanilla Windbelt, Bush Bush and Bois Neuf islands for birds, other wildlife, and the mud volcanoes and the tourist potential they represent, then they can quantify their economic value, and align conservation with market ideologies. This will then move decision makers away from environmental destruction (McCauley, 2006).

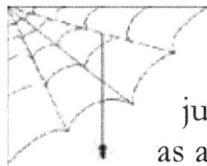

This McCauley claims is akin to saying that civil-rights advocates would have been more effective if they provided economic justifications for racial integration. Nature conservation should be framed as a moral issue and argued as such to policy-makers, says McCauley, since policy makers are just as accustomed to making decisions based on morality as on finances.

This is a difficult argument to apply to Trinidad - a complex society where authority and values have traditionally been contested. Also playing a role is the competition for economic, social and political power among the three main patriarchal groups (White, Afro, Indo - in historical sequence of arrival). Colonialism and the first post-Independent governments were based on Christian values. The predominantly Hindu government in charge during the latter stages of the Nariva conflict claimed that they did not accept these values as the norm. This reassertion of Hindu values was a surprise to those long accustomed through school and work relationships to the élite sub-group of westernised, Christianised middle class Indians. It may be that some in this sub-group had only temporarily jettisoned their Hindu traditions in order to gain political and social power through state education, and that the ones who remained Christian did not represent the larger Hindu group. This larger group consisted of Indo-Trinidadians who had reconstituted their institutions and culture in rural villages and have historically been represented by religious leaders (Mohammed, 1995) – for example coming to live in the Nariva Swamp in order to create a "new Penal." Elam (1999) calls this the Victorian definition of hybridity: in which different races continue to live separate lives and promote diverse cultural identities within the body of the hybrid state in a form of internal apartheid.

I have heard one racial group claim that the other is using population growth as a means of control-by-numbers. I have not noted any religion in Trinidad that has consistently adopted ideas of stewardship or any other religious-based ideas of environmental protection. No ethnic group including the smaller groups seem to have a coherent idea of belonging to Trinidad and conserving the environment. The culture of consumption (especially food, drink, clothes and other consumer goods) and migration abroad to seek further consumption applies to all ethnic groups. There are small groups who decline excessive consumption like some Rastas, but in my opinion there are not enough of these attitudes to make a difference.

In the past sociologists based their accounts on the assumption of exceptional traits of humans that rendered them exempt from the constraints and limits imposed by Nature (Murphy, 1995; Catton and Dunlap 1978; Dunlap and Catton, 1979). Sociologists tried to analyze man's ascent from animality and embeddedness in nature, reinforcing anthroprocentrism and self-aggrandizing the social; ignoring the ecosystem-dependence of all species including man. Murphy rightly claims that social constructions remain grounded in a dynamic ecological system even as the Earth's ecosystems become increasingly affected by human constructors.

> Human constructors who neglect the ecological system operating behind their backs, believing in the illusion of reshaping nature at will, do so at the risk of unintentional human self-destruction (Murphy, 1995).

Sociology has only recently begun to examine environmental issues and has created the concept of diachronic competition, a relationship in which contemporary well-being is achieved at the expense of our descendants (Murphy, 1995). Environmental sociology is sometimes defined as the investigation of the social dimensions of environmental problems, including the conduct of environmental politics, processes of making environmental claims and the construction of environmental knowledge (Murdoch, 2001).

Castree (1999) in his book review of Macnaghten and Urry's "Contested natures" claims that this book shows how nature and the environment are socially contested and impacted by individual and group identity, state-citizen-business relations, lay interpretations of risk and lay trust in scientific and policy elites. Political ecologists and critical geographers often cast themselves as guardians of traditional spaces and prior uses. Within this ethical framework, conservation programs are examined not for what they may accomplish in protecting endangered species or ecosystems, but to see which human groups benefit, and which others suffer (Clapp, 2004). When environmentalists claim to be safeguarding remnants of pristine nature, social science critiques depict them as evicting people and effacing cultural landscapes in order to reach an unattainable ideal of wilderness (Clapp, 2004). Which is essentially the claim that Driver (2001) makes in regard to the Northern Range. Similar arguments are made by Leach and Fairhead (2001) who take the side of the "unrepresented public" but don't quote any in their work. Murdoch (2001) wonders whether environmental sociology's attachment to the 'social' is inhibiting the emergence of a new and genuinely 'green' sub-discipline.

Murchoch writes:
> would not a truly ecological sociology necessarily need to revisit the distinction between the social and the natural so that the boundary between the two domains were, in some sense, dissolved? .If a perspective that divides society from nature is deemed to lie at the heart of the ecological crisis, should sociology be attempting to resubstantiate this supposedly damaging division?

In his book "Should trees have legal standing" Stone (1974:11) argues that nature should count jurally – to have a legally recognised worth and dignity in its own right, and not merely to serve as a means to benefit "us." He claims that for a thing to be a holder of legal rights an authoritative body must review the actions and processes of those who threaten it and three additional criteria should be satisfied. The thing can institute legal actions at its behest; second, that in determining the granting of legal relief, the court must take injury to it into account; and; third, that relief must run to the benefit of it. My problem with his argument is that for nature to have legal standing it must have a lawyer; and would therefore be dependent on the cultural values, wisdom and competence of the lawyer(s) chosen to represent it and those of the court of law with jurisdiction. Clayton (2000) claims that justice becomes more relevant in circumstances in which a desired response is scarce and in which there are citizens who ascribe moral significance and values to the environment. She goes on to state that since many resources are not renewable within reasonable time frames, this makes people more aware of the ways in which those resources are distributed. Stone (1974:16) claims that in the past natural objects have had no standing in their own right; their unique damages do not count in determining outcome; and they are not the beneficiaries of awards, but are objects for man to conquer and master and use.

Noor Mohamed Hassanali, the second President of the Republic of Trinidad and Tobago (1987-1997) was one of the few public figures to have a reputation for humility and as a Muslim did not permit alcohol in the President's House. Gerber (2002) claims that: Humility is a virtue that is helpful in a persons relationship with nature. A humble person sees value in nature and acts accordingly with the proper reverence and respect. First, humility entails an overcoming of self-absorption; the object of attention is not oneself, a walk in nature should therefore focus on what is happening in the present surroundings and not on your own concerns. Humility entails having a proper perspective on yourself (Gerber, 2002). This would include non-overestimation of yourself, not exaggerating your accomplishments, and being aware of human limitations.

This perspective is a type of self-understanding in which a person gains a proper perspective on who he is and his place in the world as a part of nature. To function, humility needs a reality greater than ourselves; a reality that inspires awe. Nature in its beauty, complexity, power and vastness provides this. Normatively, a person can understand what is valuable and can act in light of that understanding with respect and reverence. Gerber quotes another author who claims that "The person who is too ready to destroy the ancient redwoods may lack humility, not so much in the sense that he exaggerates his importance to others, but rather in the sense that he tries to avoid seeing himself as one among many natural creatures." Acts of vandalism against nature are therefore said to reflect defects in character.

Wolfe (1998) points out that several studies in ethology, field ecology, cognitive ethology, and language experiments over the past twenty years have shown that animals have the properties formerly thought to be distinctly human--language, tool use, tool making, social behaviour, altruism, non-verbal language, a hatred of boredom, an intelligent curiosity towards their environment, love for their offspring, fear of attack, deep friendships, a horror of dismemberment, a repertoire of emotions and the same capacity for exploitive violence as humans, self-awareness, the ability to engage in both deceptive and altruistic behaviour, and many other qualities thought for centuries to be exclusively human.

Some animals can be said to have moral standing independent of their cognitive or moral capacity. Beauchamp (1999) claims that there are at least two kinds of properties that qualify an animal for moral standing: having the capacity for pain and suffering, and properties of emotional deprivation. These are the properties that fuel the debates over research animals, animals in zoos and circuses and even farm animals.

The injunction to avoid causing suffering, emotional deprivation, and many other forms of harm is as well established as any principle of morality. This injunction is fashioned to protect individuals because harm is bad in itself, not because it is bad for members of a certain species or type of individual, and not because the individual is or is not a moral person. Animals have interests in avoiding harms other than those of pain, suffering, and emotional deprivation. They also have interests in not being deprived of freedom of movement and in continued life (Beauchamp, 1999).

One of the curious aspects of the Nariva conflict was that the various scientists involved never adhered to the myth of "value-free" science. This may reflect their location in a culture in which Science is not put on a pedestal and in which ethnic politics trumps all. There are quotes in interviews done by others in which Scientist-environmentalists and environmentalists did want Nariva to be free of human interference but these claims were never made in public fora (perhaps silenced by the rare firing of junior Minister Eden Shand for remarks made about squatters) and these occasionally proclaimed beliefs did not stop these same scientists-environmentalists from writing reports on the sustainable use of the Swamp for internal and external audiences.

Jacques (2006) claims that some proponents of "wise use" are actually environmental skeptics. Skeptics believe that the domination of nature was necessary for the fantastic success of modernity, which has provided humanity with the progress and affluence our pre-modern predecessors could only have dreamed of. This deep or skeptical anthropocentrism holds an extreme "exemptionalist" perspective that sees humans as fully exempt from ecological principles, influences and limits. People can thrive without nature and a growing distance between non-human nature and civilization is necessary for a good society (Jacques, 2006).

Skeptics assert that there are no environmental problems that threaten environmental sustainability, and that the environmental movement is obstructing human progress (arguments that I have heard in Trinidad and Tobago). Environmental skepticism is sometimes sympathetic to "free market environmentalism," which prefers market-based rather than state-based solutions to environmental problems which they admit truly exist. Jacques claims that skeptics (often very faithfully politically conservative) use various strategies including the media (i.e. labeling alternative views as junk science and fear mongering) to create significant levels of political conflict within epistemic communities in order to stall protective environmental policy rather than trying to debate environmental claims and letting the "best science prevail."

Social scientists seemed to have turned a feminist lens on the term "junk science" which they say is science that simply contradicts a capitalistic goal of accumulation of wealth (i.e the term is a political trope). Consequently, the term "junk science" has very little to do with science or fraud, but more to do with whom that science serves - the status quo system of accumulation and power for the consumptive elite in the Global North (and their imitators).

Therefore the dominant social paradigm:
   (1) commitment to limited government and less planning and regulation,
   (2) support for free enterprise and economic growth,
   (3) devotion to private property rights and individualism,
   (4) faith in the efficacy of science and technology and future abundance

is at the root of the ecological crisis; which explains why so much effort and so many resources are poured into the political struggles of the politically conservative environmental sceptics.

Hettinger (2002) tries to articulate a positive role for humans in the natural world:

> An adequate environmental philosophy must allow that human beings belong on the planet too, and it must articulate how it is possible for us to respect nature while continuing to be human. We need to conceive of a constructive human/ nature relationship that allows us to "imagine giving more to the world around us than the gift of our mere absence." What is needed if humans are to have something other than a purely negative and harmful role with respect to nature is a distinction between human alteration of nature and human domination of Nature. We need to conceive of certain types of human uses of nature as not abusive.

Hettinger gives sustainable forestry as an example. He claims that human alterations can be nature respecting and need not be purely anthropocentric in an instrumental sense. This will allow humans to use nature as a means without necessarily using it as a mere means (2002). Jacques (2006) quotes research suggesting that humans need to replace open privileges with an expanded set of responsibilities "founded on the principles of membership and citizenship in—rather than dominion and exploitation of—the community of nature."

Governance - Background

The Nariva Swamp, 6234 hectares, was declared to be a forest reserve in 1954. The Bush Bush section of the Nariva Swamp (3,480 acres) is an area of high ground that was declared as a wildlife sanctuary in 1968, and a prohibited area in 1989 by Dr. Keith Rowley (legal notice no 78 by then Minster of Agriculture, Land and Marine Resources). Goolcharan and Parbatee Jabar filed a constitutional motion against this legal notice of the state re "the right to enjoyment of property" through their lawyer Ramesh Lawrence Maharaj (Wildlife Section, 1993).

The site was thus reserved as a local and international research centre, and in theory no hunting or harvesting was allowed on the site. The Trinidad Regional Virus Lab (TRVL) (now CAREC) conducted research on arboviruses there in past decades. The Nariva Swamp is protected by 3 main pieces of legislation: the Forests Act, Chapter 66: 01; the Conservation of Wildlife Act, Chapter 67: 01; the State Lands Act, Chapter 57: 01. Offences taken to court are usually related to wildlife poaching and tree felling. This has not been entirely successful and encroachment by squatters in on going (Ramsar, 1996). Agriculture consists of cutting, burning and planting, followed by abandonment in favour of newly cleared land (Ramsar, 1996). The Nariva Swamp has been threatened in the past by illegal squatting; the conversion of land to cannabis and rice farming, illegal grazing of livestock in the game sanctuary, overfishing and illegal timber harvesting, illegal hunting and excessive trapping of birds for the pet trade (Ramsar, 1996). From 1997 – 98 $3 million worth of marijuana grown on Bois Neuf island was burnt by the Organised Crime and Narcotics Unit (Trinidad Guardian Oct 14, 1998 photo). Similar operations were carried out in 1987 on Bois Neuf Hill by National Security helicopters and the costs involved could have used for support of the Wildlife Section instead. Was it a "masculinity issue" or an IMF dictate to use resources for army surveillance than have weekly surveillance by state employees?

This study of governance issues associated with the Nariva Swamp is part of a larger study coordinated by The Centre for Gender and Development Studies, (CG&DS), UWI. The overall research acts as a means to develop the concepts of the terms of island sustainability, equity, livelihood and governance for Trinidad and Tobago. The CG&DS is linked to the ISLE (Island Sustainability Livelihood and Equity) programme, which is an integrated programme that has the sustainable development of island states as its primary research focus. The ISLE program began in 1995, and is funded by the Canadian International Development Agency (CIDA).

This document is divided into 4 parts. The first part consists of a gendered analysis of the interviews conducted with various stakeholders and interested parties in the Nariva Swamp issue from July to September 1999. Stakeholders are people or groups involved in implementing proposed policies and those who are directly or indirectly impacted by policy. This analysis is combined with an analysis of the secondary data collected over the same period on the policy and governance decisions taken towards the Swamp.

Aims of the study: Governance and policy issues

This study examines the history of governance and policy issues related to the Nariva wetlands and surrounding areas and the countervailing interests of various stakeholders. This exploration will incorporate a gender analysis. It includes an examination of whether the previous policy(s) of the Government of the Republic of Trinidad and Tobago (GORTT) can be construed as gendered phenomena and if so, what are the implications of this?

This examination will include an analysis of the stakeholders in the Nariva issues and the power differentials between them.

The study is based on documentation and evaluation of state policy toward agricultural resource use and settlement in the Nariva area (e.g. agricultural policy, settlement policy, infrastructural development, tourism policy, political context, allocation of land rights).

Research questions associated with this governance component are listed below:
• Is there a crisis in leadership and governance in Trinidad and Tobago on environmental issues that environmental organisations are seeking to fill through links to international organisations and funding agencies?

Has there been a historical predisposition to favour commercial use of the swamp rather than ecologically sustainable use? And if so is this predisposition a gendered one?

• Has the granting of international recognition to Nariva as a Ramsar site affected the ecological status of the swamp, the political status of the swamp, the livelihood of the communities, the type of research being conducted, the beneficiaries of research funding?

• What are the scientific relations of power, and current environmental ideologies and discourses that affect the Nariva swamp?

Governance comprises of State, local and community levels. The significance of the macro level is its power to make things happen. It is the level at which decisions are made for the entire nation, and where international events and forces are mediated for the nation (FAO-SEAGA). Although governance comprises of State, local and community levels, only the State level could be addressed given the time factor and the limited resources provided for the study.

How the study was conducted

A review of the secondary literature was made. The literature review included rice production, gender analysis, local environmental issues, governance issues and all previous documents related to the Nariva Swamp, from the UWI library and the library of the Ministry of Agriculture at St. Clair. Newspaper clippings relevant to the Nariva issue and environmental issues were collected from various sources including the two libraries mentioned above.

Fig 4. Existing institutional and administrative framework for Nariva Swamp (source: IMA, 1999)

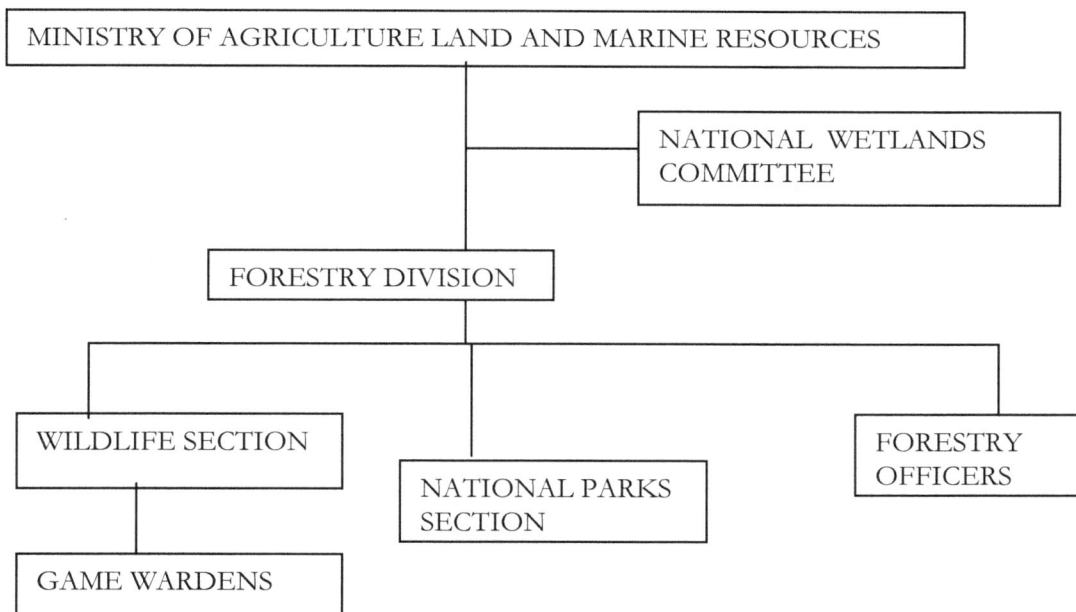

Open-ended interviews were held with the stakeholders involved in the Nariva issue listed below. The stakeholders were asked about their role in the Nariva issue and their views on the matter. The interviews took place at the homes or work places of the people concerned. The interviews took place from July to September 1999.

The Ministry of Agriculture, Land and Marine Resources (MALMR) and the Land and Surveys Division are major stakeholders but only Ms. Robyn Cross, of the National Parks/Wildlife Section, Forestry Division, MALMR and Dr. Carol James, formerly Head of the Wildlife Section, currently with the UNDP-GEF were interviewed from that Ministry. These two actors were very much involved in the Nariva issue. Attempts to also interview Ms. Nathai-Gyan from the National Parks/Wildlife Section were not successful.

o Three former Ministers of Agriculture/Environment were interviewed, Mr. Kamaluddin Mohammed (First PNM government up to 1985), Mr. Lincoln Myers (1986 – 1991) and Dr. Brinsley Samaroo (1995 – 2000). They were three of five involved in the Nariva Swamp issue. Only Dr. Samaroo was interviewed in the context of this study, the two others were interviewed for a previous study (Lans, 1996) and their comments are included in the body of the study.

o Ms. Molly Gaskin, and Ms. Karilyn Shephard of the Pointe á Pierre Wildfowl Trust were very much involved as environmental activists in the Nariva conflict. Ms. Karilyn Shephard is also a member of the Council of Presidents of the Environment (COPE).

o Three members of the Akaloo family, the most visible and publicly known large rice farmers were interviewed. Theresa Akaloo was president of the Trinidad and Tobago Rice Growers Association (TIRGA).

o The Institute of Marine Affairs (IMA) was visited but none of the staff was formally interviewed.

o Prof. P.R. Bacon of the University of the West Indies was interviewed since he has done some consultancy work on the Nariva Swamp, and has been involved in the issue from the beginning.

o Ms. Sylvia Kacal, member of the Caribbean Forestry Conservation Association (CFCA) has done environmental consultancy work on the Nariva Swamp and was interviewed in that capacity.

26

- Mr. Eden Shand of the CFCA is an environmental consultant and former junior Minister of Environment and has well known views on the Nariva Swamp conflict.

- Dr. Victor Quesnel, is a former head of the Trinidad and Tobago Field Naturalists Club and was interviewed on the role of the Club in the Nariva issue and the Club's general stance towards environmental activism.

- Mr. Walters from the National Flour Mills.

- A former member of the Agricultural Development Bank (ADB) was interviewed previous to this study and his comments are included as secondary material. He asked not to be identified.

- The library of the Environmental Management Authority (EMA) was visited and a senior male member of staff was interviewed for a previous study. Material from this interview is included as secondary material.

- Mr. Stephen Broadbridge was interviewed as an ecotourism operator (Caribbean Discovery Tours) who conducts tours to the Nariva Swamp.

- An environmental lawyer was interviewed previous to this study and his comments are included as part of the secondary material. He asked not to be identified.

- Two male and one female agricultural consultant who were not directly involved in the Nariva issue but had broad knowledge of agriculture, economics and politics were interviewed to give some context to the study. These were previously known to the author and known to talk freely rather than give socially correct responses. They asked not to be identified. Extracts are taken from most of the interviews to illustrate different points. It was not considered necessary to always identify the authors of these quotes.

- In addition to the comments of the Project Coordinators comments on a previous draft were also obtained from Dr. Carol James and Dr. Brinsley Samaroo.

Rice in Trinidad Historical review and perspective

Production

A survey conducted in 1981 indicated that 99% of rice farms had an average size of 1.3 acres (0.51 hectares) and manual cultivation was used. In 1954, 45% of rice consumption was produced locally but this decreased to 22% and 12.6% in 1981 and 1987. The cultivated area decreased from 8,000 hectares in 1951 to 4,533 hectares in 1981. The trend of declining acreage and production was reversed in the 1980s, especially since 1986. By 1990, the total land area devoted to rice production was 6,200 hectares of which 2,000 hectares were occupied by large farmers (>50 hectares). This includes Caroni (1975) Ltd. with 900 hectares. During the period 1986 - 1990, paddy production increased by over 400% from 2.4 Mn kg. to 14 Mn kg. Small farmers were the leading suppliers of paddy to the Rice Mill averaging 62.6% followed by Caroni and Large farmers with 28.7% and 8.7% respectively.

For 1991, production was 17.2 Mn kg. and reached an all time high of 21.9 Mn kg. at the end of 1992. This represented an increase of 27.3% on 1991 output. Large and small farmers contributed 70.7%, and Caroni 29.3%. Local rice production has shown a parallel and similar increase in production as paddy, increasing by 800% during the period 1986 - 1992. Production was 1.44 Mn Kg. in 1986 and 13.14 Mn kg. in 1992. The local industry increased its market share from a meager 5% in 1986 to 31% in 1992.

Much of the increase was due to the advent of the Central Rice Mill and a guaranteed price for paddy, aided of course by the deteriorating national economic conditions which resulted in an influx of labour into the agricultural sector. As a result rice production has become much less subsistence and more commercial.

The change has also resulted in some improvements in the technology of production. Caroni (1975) Ltd. and the large farmers are completely mechanised including the use of aircraft for sowing, application of fertilisers and plant protection. The farming systems of the small farmers is still heavily manual though tillage and threshing operations are mechanised. In 1993, local production was estimated to be 20% of the demand for rice. The long term achievable target is estimated at 75% or 30,000 tonnes of milled rice. To achieve this target requires an additional 7,000 hectares of double cropped rice with an average yield of 4.0 tonnes/hectares. One escalating problem is the extent of squatting associated with the activities of particularly the large private farmers, many of whom operate in the Plum Mitan area on the fringes of the Nariva Swamp.

Marketing

The National Flour Mills (NFM) has the responsibility to purchase all locally grown paddy through the Rice Mill at Carlsen Field. Paddy is bought at $1.96/kg from small farmers and $1.76/kg from large farmers and Caroni (1975) Ltd. Farmers are penalized for supplying paddy with a moisture content above 17%.

NFM also has a monopoly with respect to the importation of rice into the country, and has some influence in the setting of the retail price of rice. The retail price of rice is price-controlled and determined by the Prices Control Commission. Loose white rice is sold at $1.91 per kg while the packaged rice fetches a higher price. The profits from the rice importation operation are utilised in support of the subsidy for domestic paddy purchased. NFM suffers a loss on the production of local rice, which except for paddy purchased from Caroni (1975) Ltd., is generally very poor and unsuitable for human consumption, and has to be sold at a much lower price to pet food manufacturers. Thus increased output by small farmers has negatively affected NFM's profit margin. The local rice industry has reached the stage where paddy production is increasing at a rapid rate and is causing a serious financial burden on the NFM. Grading farmers' paddy would assist NFM in alleviating its losses because they are mandated to purchase paddy regardless of quality.

Guaranteed Price and Price Support Programme (Paddy)

The period 1986 - 1991 saw a total of $103 Md being paid to paddy growers under the guaranteed price and price support programme. This represented approximately 22.7% of total payment made for all commodities. Paddy ranks second after sugarcane in this programme. Payment for paddy from growers by NFM increased from $5.3 Mn in 1986 to $25.0 Mn in 1991. This is an increase of over 300%. For 1992 payments made to rice farmers under this programme were $23.0 Mn. This represented an 8% decline in payments as compared to 1991.

Table 1. Domestic production of rice paddy (000 KG.)

FARMING TYPE	1986	1987	1988	1989	1990	1991	1992
CARONI	39.2	1919.2	1970.1	3843.3	4774.8	5642.0	6418.2
LARGE	91.4	362.2	652.5	1339.2	1100.1	10584.5	}15471.4
SMALL	2231.8	3309.6	3705.1	3860.9	8168.5	}	}
TOTAL	2362.4	5591.0	6327.7	9043.5	14043.4	16190.5	21889.6
IMPORTS	29.4 Mn kg.					21.6 Mn kg.	29.89 Mn kg

Table 2.Paddy yield

FARMER	AVG. YIELD (tons/hectares)	COST OF PRODUCTION OF PADDY ($/KG.)	COST OF PRODUCTION (PADDY)/TONNE (US$)
CARONI	3	1.43 - 1.73	
LARGE	2.5	1.43 - 1.73	
SMALL	2.5	1.49 - 1.93	
INDONESIA			84
USA			132
GUYANA			124
BELIZE			153
TRINIDAD			309

Performance of the Sector - An Overview

In 1993, local paddy production was 16.2 Mn kg (MALMR, 1995: 11). This represented a decline in output of approximately 26% on the 1992 output of 21.9 Mn kg. This was the first time in eight consecutive years since 1986 that paddy production had registered a decline. Thus, despite the gains that the country has made in rice production, it remains a net rice importer. In 1993, rice imports amounted to 59.8 Mn kg. This represented an increase of approximately 46% on 1992 rice imports of 40.80 Mn kg. This rise in imports was a mirror reflection of the decline experienced in local paddy production during the 1993 crop. The United States remains the major source of our rice imports supplying 96.7% (MALMR, 1995).

Brief history of issues related to the Nariva Swamp

Historically speaking the Nariva Swamp was not seen as a conservation site but was seen in macro-economic terms as a potential energy site. This is illustrated in a National Radio and TV broadcast called 'An up to date account of the energy situation' given on the 8 May 1974. In this broadcast Prime Minister Dr. Eric Williams made the following comment:

"We await the arrival of the experts whom we have requested from the United Nations for seismic aeromagnetic survey, which will give us information both on mineral resources other than hydrocarbons for the country as a whole as well as on potential oil resources in the following four locations:
(1) the Nariva Swamp
(2) specific areas in the south-west peninsula
(3) the area of the Central Range particularly around Tabaquite and Mahaica
(4) the Laventille Swamp (Sutton, 1981)

Four years earlier in another broadcast on " National Reconstruction, 30 June 1970, Dr. Williams again commented on the Swamp as a non-conservation site but fell under structural land reform policy:

"I have always myself thought, with the increasing congestion of our urban areas, that a new town could be developed in the eastern part of the country in relation to the proposed drainage of the Nariva Swamp. These are just ideas. The young people may have other ideas. I await their constructive proposals (Sutton, 1981).

Indirect threats to the Swamp include land alienation. Agricultural land is allowed to go to other uses and farmers then apply for new State lands including Swamps. MacMillan (1967) gives a historical perspective on this point for Aranjuez:

'Even if the gardeners succeed in 'holding their own' socially and economically in Aranjuez, the future of the agricultural land is not entirely secure. The value of land for building purposes is about $15,000 per acre: the land owners receive at the moment a maximum of $10 per acre annual rent, and are expected to maintain the infra-structure. The nation's planners have allowed other highly productive areas to be swallowed up by Port of Spain, and the pressure on them to permit the owners of the Estate to build at Aranjuez are very high. The returns from market gardening are good, but can hardly be equated with those from real property in an inflated market, and so the only way the agricultural sector can be preserved is by law' (MacMillan, 1967).

The following history is adapted from several sources but mainly from Mootoosingh (1979).

In 1891, the Society for the Study of Natural History was established. This Society became the Trinidad and Tobago Field Naturalists Club, which is still active in environmental issues, but is not an activist organisation.

The first recorded local conservation activity took place in 1765, when the Main Ridge in Tobago was set aside as the first forest reserve in the New World. In 1900, the creation of twelve Forest Reserves was suggested in a report by Deputy Conservator of the Indian Forest Service, F. Lodge and four years later in 1904, the first Forest Reserves in Trinidad were set aside. In 1901, the Forestry Branch of the Crown Lands Department was established. Seventeen years later, in 1918, the Forestry Branch became the Forest Department and Officers were appointed. In 1960, the Forest Department was integrated into the Ministry of Agriculture, Lands and Fisheries and became the Forestry Division. Also in 1960 was the initial Planning Ordinance.

The Manzanilla Windbelt, of 1782.2 hectares located close to the Nariva Swamp was declared a demarcated Forest Reserve in 1922. Brigand Hill, 127.9 hectares, which is on the boundary of the Nariva Swamp, was declared a demarcated Forest Reserve in 1925. New Forestry reserves were created and laws were revised until 1960.

In the 1920s, the reclamation of Caroni swamp was attempted but in 1953, the Caroni Swamp was established as a Bird Sanctuary and the Swamp was put under the full protection of a Wildlife Warden in 1963. Bacon and Mahadeo (1999) claimed that attempts to revitalize the Cipriani Reclamation Scheme were made in the 1940s and

1950s but it scheme was abandoned as a failure in 1954, but the swamp had become damaged by increased salinity caused by the projects.

Caroni was the first protected wetland; other swamps were converted into rice production as early as 1954 when the Colonial Government established the Plum Mitan rice scheme, and the Fishing Pond and Oropouche Lagoon schemes. Taitt (1999) claims that 442 of 562 rice plots laid out by government in the Oropouche Lagoon were taken by peasants in 1917 and that half-acre blocks were taken in Nariva lagoon the next year.

Taitt also claims that there were 5000 fewer acres under rice in 1918 but production remained the same and that the growers had abandoned older lands for the new land which may account for the similarity in production levels. The warden of Naparima of the time made repeated calls for the Oropouche Lagoon to be drained for rice production. Bacon and Mahadeo (1999) wrote that the Oropuche lagoon reclamation was restarted in the 1950s, but there was rapid decline in the infrastructure and in soil quality. In 1998 less than one-third of the reclaimed area was still in production and salt tolerant plants were evidence of the soil salinity.

A more contemporary suggestion for development of the Nariva Swamp came from the FAO (1957) report. The FAO Report to the GORTT on the Reclamation of the Caroni, Oropouche and Nariva areas for rice and other agricultural production revealed that the soil in the lower regions of the Swamp was prone to shrinkage, was of poor quality and not worth reclaiming.

The study recommended the improvement of the Plum Mitan rice scheme, which was established by the Colonial Government in 1954 but there were cautions on the soil deterioration in the Swamp basin. They also recommended the establishment of two polders on the more elevated areas in the western section of the swamp. The polders were of 1320 hectares and 520 hectares with the provision for adequate drainage through a main drain exiting to the Nariva Swamp close to the mouth. The government of Trinidad and Tobago did implement the Plum Mitan Rice Scheme in the 1950s. This decision was later reinforced by the rehabilitation study of Netherlands Engineering Consultants (NEDECO, 1983). The Plum Mitan Rice Scheme was meant to provide small land assignments (2 hectares to 5 hectares) to family farms. The area is approximately 375 hectares, of which one-third is in use each year (Keeler and Pemberton, 1996).

In January 1966, the Overseas Technical Co-operation Agency (O.C.T.A) of Japan visited Trinidad. They then conducted a reconnaissance survey in September 1967. A feasibility study in 1969 and a development plan for the Nariva Swamp followed this. The study claimed that reclamation of the entire Swamp for rice was feasible and economically viable. The O.C.T.A agricultural development scheme is for rice in the wet season with such crops as soybeans and maize during the dry season.

In 1934, the first Wild Animals and Birds (Protection) Ordinance (Chapter 25, No. 27) set aside certain forest areas as reserves where hunting was prohibited. Twenty years in 1958, there was a debate in the House of Representatives about the change in the Game laws to wildlife protection laws. The 1958 Wildlife Conservation Ordinance no. 16 included the establishment of a Wildlife Conservation Committee which served as an advisory Committee to the Minister of Agriculture, Lands and Fisheries.

In 1954, the Nariva Windbelt Forest Reserve of 6,267 acres was declared under the Forests Act on March 18 1954. This designation gives the Forestry Division the authority to manage the area with reference to felling of trees, damage by negligence in felling any tree or dragging any timber, fires, and forest produce (CFCA, 1997). The year after the establishment of the Nariva Windbelt Forest Reserve (1955) the Manzanilla Extension, 383.2 hectares was declared a demarcated Forest Reserve.

Scientist T.H.G. Aitken proposed the Bush Bush wildlife sanctuary in the Nariva Swamp as a nature reserve in 1960 (Bacon et al., 1979). In 1962, the International Council for Bird Preservation raised a protest against proposed logging operations by the Forestry Division in the Nariva Swamp; the Council protested that it would reduce the high bird diversity in the area (Bacon et al., 1979). At the end of his study of parrots and macaws, scientists Dr. F. Nottebohm and Carl Carlozzi recommended the complete legal protection of the Bush Bush and Bois Neuf islands for the birds and other wildlife, the mud volcanoes on Bois Neuf and the tourist potential they contained.

Bonadie and Bacon (1998) confirmed that roosting sites for orange-winged parrots (*Amazona amazonica*) and red-bellied macaws (*Ara manilata* (Bodd.)) were concentrated in *Roystonea* and *Mauritia* palm stands in the Nariva Swamp and they only counted 136 parrots (a reduction from 600 in 1969) and 224 macaws. The Conservation Ordinance allows orange-winged parrots to be shot as crop pests, so that if the palm swamp forest is eliminated they will become greater pests of cocoa and crops and will face greater levels of irate shooting. Parrots and macaws fed on seven plant species with the major concentration of feeding on *Mauritia setigera* and *Roystonea oleracea* palm fruit. The third psittacine species observed in the swamp were green-rumped parrotlets (*Forpus passerinus* Lafr.).

As a result of the public interest and a grant of $5000 U.S. from the New York Zooloogical Society, the Bush Bush area was declared a Wildlife Sanctuary on 16th July 1968 (Bacon et al., 1979). In recognition of this interest, in July 1968, the Trinidad and Tobago Tourist Board held a meeting with the Forestry Division on the potential of the mouth of the Nariva River and its eastern bank for tourism. Six years later in 1974, the Tourist Board offered financial aid of $7000 to clear and maintain the Bush Bush canal to allow easier access. However, this money was never allocated to the Forestry Division for this purpose (Bacon et al., 1979).

Even though sanctuaries had been established in the Nariva Swamp, other uses for the area were still being planned. For example in 1970 the O.C.T.A plan for drainage and agricultural development of the Nariva swamp recommended settlement of 640 new families in 3 new villages in the Swamp basin. Besides rice the plan recommended corn and soya and grazing on the higher ground. However the 1972 Surveys Division Maps for the Land Capability Classification Studies suggested that Nariva Swamp soils were unsuitable for agriculture and should be left under tree crops and forest.

Despite the unsuitability of the soil it is claimed that in the mid-1970s, GORTT assisted squatters in Kernahan and Cascadoux with access roads and channel maintenance. These residents came from Penal, Debe and Rio Claro and some also have land and houses in those places and live in the swamp temporarily (Cross et al., 1999; Maharaj, 2000; Doodhai, 2000). As stated above the Colonial Government established the Plum Mitan rice scheme in 1954. In 1976/77 there was a plan by MALMR to revitalize 1400 acres in Plum Mitan to produce 2200 lbs rice/ acre or 3,080,000 lbs /annum. 1500 acres at Kernahan /Cascadoux were to produce 3,300,000 lbs/ annum.

The report by Bacon et al. (1979) filled in some of the ecological gaps in the FAO and O.C.T.A (1967, 1970) documents. The Department of Zoology conducted the research. The scientists felt that the original plan did not pay any attention to the ecology of the area or the environmental impacts. Bacon et al. (1979) reported that the Nariva Swamp was not considered as a major plant resource production area but as largely a wasteland (pg. 127). The report went on to say that Government saw an economic future for the Swamp only when reclaimed for agriculture. The scientists claimed that the great variability of the vegetation, its patchy distribution, its inaccessibility and the discomfort of working in swampy conditions all contributed to the low level of exploitation of what they called the minor plant resources and that the possibility existed for considerable resource improvement.

"In addition to direct exploitation, the value of the vegetation in its natural condition requires greater recognition" (pg. 127, 128) since the vegetation provides food for major faunal resources and releases large quantities of nutrients and detritus to neighbouring ecosystems. They argued that the conservation of the natural vegetation was essential to preserve the productivity of the Swamp. Since the Swamp ecosystem depended on the drainage from the western watershed, maintenance of the forest there was important to the continued health of the Swamp. The Zoologists used Chalmers concept of social forestry to underline the importance of developing the Nariva Swamp in the context of the total social development of the east Trinidad and to sustain reclamation agriculture. They reported that logs of Cedar and Crappo had been taken from Bois Neuf and that Matchwood was taken from the Wildlife sanctuary.

They projected that the yield from the windbelt of 1 m cubed/hectares/annum would be low (pg. 129). From the ecological or environmental point of view the "protective" role of forests must also be acknowledged (assisting in the protection of inland areas from the sea and in the development of new land along the coastline). They gave some potential uses of various plants including medicines, and grasses for dry season fodder. They recommended that the Nariva Swamp forest areas should not be reclaimed, but should be conserved and managed intensively as plantation forests concentrating on the more valuable timber and food crop species. Development of the Nariva Swamp may disrupt animal species of present commercial importance. Management of the Swamp in its natural condition could bring high economic returns through production of fish, crustacea, shellfish and game, without the uncertainties attached to a wetlands reclamation scheme. There were a large number of edible invertebrates and vertebrates present and it was suggested that the wise use of these natural faunal resources might in the long term bring greater economic returns with fewer potential problems than the proposed rice growing scheme (pg. 145).

The conservation of the number of rare and endangered animals present had potential to bring economic benefits through educational and recreational use. The presence of nuisance insects and potential crop pests, and their control without causing environmental damage, are serious constraints on development of the Swamp. Therefore they recommended that the area scheduled for rice cultivation should be reduced to allow greater exploitation of the Nariva Swamp fisheries.

Their modifications of the O.C.T.A plan included the revitalisation of the Plum Mitan rice project (800 hectares), together with the redevelopment of the Kernahan area (800 hectares) and the creation of a polder of 1600 hectares south of the Plum Mitan rice project. The Cocal reservoir was supposed to be built so as not to affect the Bush-Bush area. The Nariva regulating reservoir was to be expanded to cover all low-lying Swamp ground.

The recommendations of Bacon et al. (1979) included a maximization of biological resources: 4000 acres for rice, 4000 for cattle, 8000 acres for fisheries, a Cocal Reservoir and the maintenance of the Wildlife Sanctuary. The impacts of the changes proposed in the O.C.T.A. Development Plan (1970) are summarised in Table 3.

Table 3. Impacts of the O.C.T.A Development Proposals (Bacon et al. 1979, 266)

PROPOSED CHANGE	POSSIBLE IMPACTS	RECOMMENDED ACTION
1. Nariva River Closure	Upset coastal stability loss of fisheries	Re-investigate.
2. Flood water removal (Cocal Canal)	Upset basic ecology of area. Water loss.	Continue natural flooding of non-agricultural areas.
3. Floodwater storage (Cocal reservoir	Increase fish habitat. Seasonal isolation of Bush Bush and Bois Neuf	Supported.
4. Construction of Cocal embankment.	Damage to Sanctuary, increase access.	Move north of Bush Bush and Bois Neuf.
5. Forest clearance for livestock on S-W watershed area.	Soil erosion, silting and eutrophication of Cocal Reservoir. Loss of forest, production of poor pasture.	Maintain forest cover. Develop livestock area in Swamp basin.
6. Polder drainage.	Soil deterioration, loss of fisheries.	Intensive soil and water conservation. Construction of polder canals to maintain fishing.
7. Nariva Regulating Reservoir.	Stagnation, salination and isolation of fish stocks.	Maintain natural water regime and access to other areas by aquatic organisms.
8. New village settlements.	Pollution, spread of disease, loss of cultivable land.	Remove from plan. Involve already existing communities.

Two aquaculture projects were submitted to GORTT by private agencies for the Nariva Swamp. The FAO was invited in 1984 by MALMR for assistance in appraising the aquaculture potential of the Swamp. The two projects were the conversion of 2,000 hectares for marine shrimp culture and commercial fishing of cascadura and the giant freshwater prawn on 80 hectares (Deepsea Industries Ltd.). The first project was withdrawn since it involved introduction of seawater into the swamp. The 1984 Mission recommended a technical assessment, which was done by Mr. P.G. Padlan, Senior Fisheries Officer of UNDP/FAO and Dr. P. Bacon of UWI, Jamaica as Wetland Ecologist. The FAO (1985) study recommended the development of aquaculture as part of the rehabilitation of the Nariva Swamp. The study identified the peat soils and unripe clays classified by NEDECO as unsuitable for agriculture as potential areas for aquaculture projects. The Bush Bush sanctuary was recognised and an environmental impact assessment of the proposed projects was included. The system was for deep water polyculture in excavated earthen ponds with *Tilapia nilotica* (tilapia), cascadura, coscorob and *Ctenopharyngodon idella* (grass carp). Both the tilapia and the grass carp would have had to be introduced into the country. Murray et al. (1982) claim that the 1985 FAO mission recommended that Navet Dam rather than Nariva swamp be used.

The reclamation of Nariva for agriculture remained in the planning stages with a new study by NEDECO, which was a summary and review of previous studies on reclamation of Nariva Swamp published in 1981. In 1983, NEDECO produced a *Final Report Phase 1: Investigations of the development of the Nariva Swamp* that included agricultural development for rice farming on the existing 370 hectares in Plum Mitan and 450 hectares in the Cocal-Kernahan areas. They also included 1200 hectares of what they called a Biche Bois Neuf polder (roughly corresponding to the FAO 1957 Polder 1), which they gave the lowest priority to.

In 1991 the Draft Final Report for the Agristudio Reconnaissance study for the extension of the Plum Mitan Scheme was published. Agristudio recommended the expansion of the Plum Mitan rice project to other areas of the Swamp suitable for irrigation development. These included areas already largely and illegally cultivated: 100 hectares in Petit Pool, 1200 hectares in Biche Bois Neuf (Block B) and 700 hectares in the Cocal-Kernahan area.

They recommended the creation of a 200 hectares buffer zone between the Biche Bois Neuf reclamation area and the Bush Bush sanctuary. Agristudio reviewed the previous studies and claimed that the construction of the main drain recommended by the FAO (1957) study would drain water into the Swamp in the dry season if there were no regulating devices put in place. They also felt that the drain would encourage salt water intrusion. This study criticised the O.C.T.A (1967) study for proposing to completely alter the Nariva Swamp. The proposed embankment from O.C.T.A (1967) study was criticised since it would have been built on peaty sub-soil. They also felt that the irrigation component was insufficient. Agristudio felt that UWI's plan to construct the Cocal reservoir was inadequate since it would involve a long embankment built on soft peaty soils.

In February 1992, a team of consultants prepared a study on the feasibility of rehabilitation and expansion of the Plum Mitan Rice Scheme up to 3,000 hectares Details of the engineering and hydrology were itemized and there is a proposed cropping pattern based on water utilization and efficiency. The proposed farm size is 3 hectares of which 2.5 hectares will be solely for rice production and 0.5 hectares for vegetable production.

In 1983 the National Physical Development Plan was introduced into Parliament. This plan contained a recommendation for a growth pole in Guayaguayare-Galeota. As part of this growth pole the "undeveloped Nariva Swamp was to be converted into 9000 acres for intensive farming, 7500 acres for livestock rearing. Cultivation of idle lands of good agricultural potential was to form the basis of sizeable food processing and other agro-based industry." This Plan was debated and approved in 1984.

It was with full knowledge of the plans for rice production that the rice farmer /squatter Jury ignored quit notices for Bush Bush sanctuary in 1984. The Wildlife Section (1993) claimed that he was squatting in a building belonging to the Trinidad Regional Virus Lab and that the legal case against him was adjourned by the Rio Claro Magistrates Court ten times between 1987 and 1993. It was also in this context that large-scale rice farmers the Akaloos' moved to squat and plant rice in the Nariva Swamp in 1986. Two years later, 1988, the Draft Public Sector Investment Programme laid in Parliament by Planning and Mobilisation Minister Winston Dookeran, included expanded rice production for Plum Mitan, according to large-scale rice farmer Theresa Akaloo.

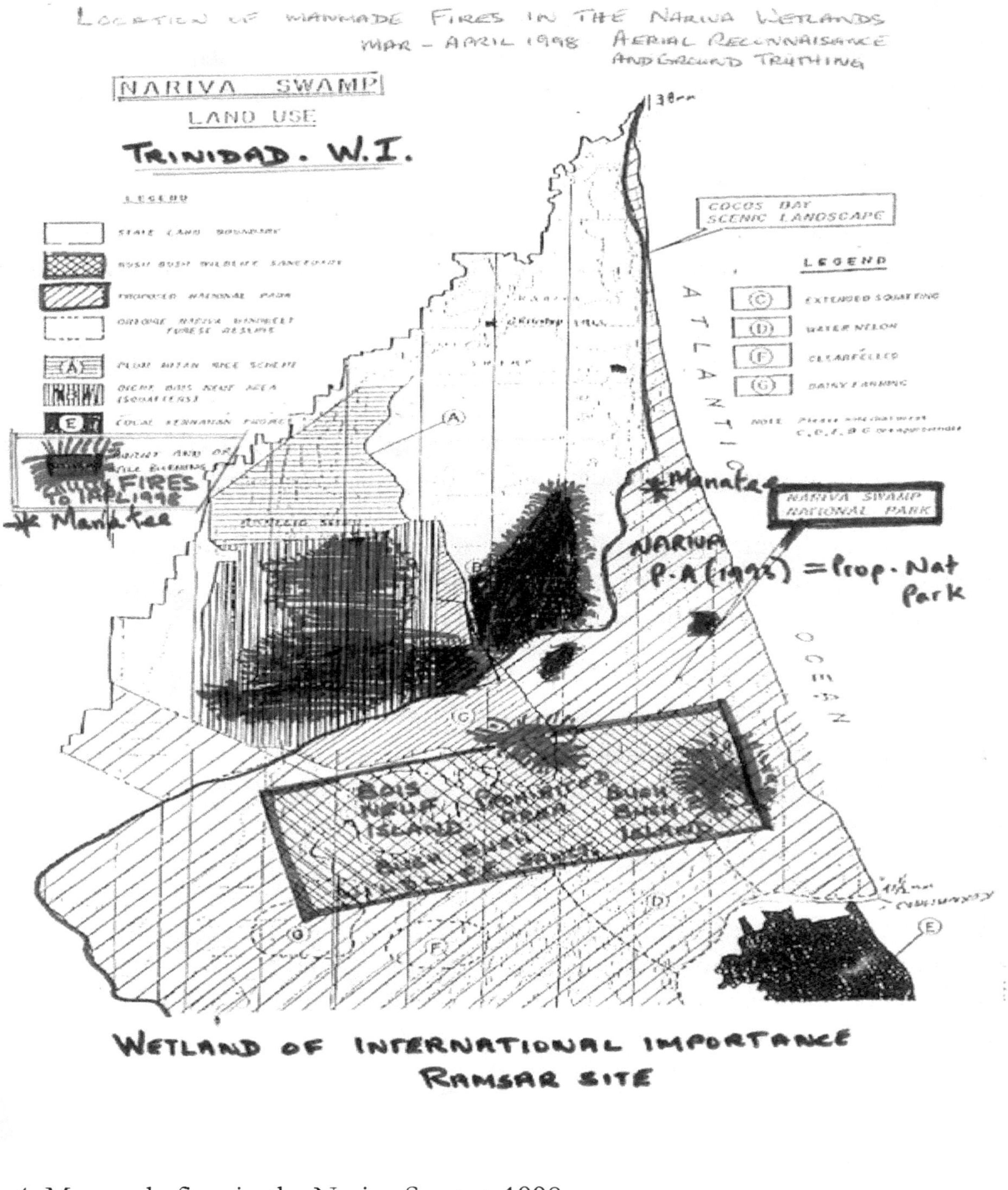

Fig 4. Manmade fires in the Nariva Swamp 1998

For decades the Swamp has been the centre of concern and controversy because of the real conflict between legal and illegal commercial use of the Swamp (logging, rice production, fishing) and the ecological and physical sustainability of the Swamp. The controversy escalated when agricultural planners decided to provide a subsidy for rice growers in mid-1980s, to stimulate rice production and achieve some level of self-sufficiency. The subsidy served as an incentive for large-scale producers to convert approximately Sector B of the Swamp into commercial rice production.

Table 4. Note on producer subsidy equivalents (from MALMR).

CROP	%PSE	%CSE	COMMENTS
SUGAR	71.8	59.5	domestic consumers supporting the industry by 60% of their expenditure on sugar
RICE	69	31.7	consumers paying about one-third of their total expenditure on rice in supporting the producers of rice
COCOA	-17.7	-2.36	producers being taxed
COFFEE	86.7		
CITRUS	-329.3		
CABBAGE	-13.1	-32.3	
TOMATO	-57.2	-79.6	
MILK	70	25.8	
BEEF	46.6		
BROILERS	66.5	66.4	
SHEEP	50.9	50.9	
PORK	71	43.2	

From 1987, Nathai-Gyan (1997) estimates that 80% of the Biche-Bois Neuf area (sector B) was converted to rice cultivation. These growers had a negative impact on the Nariva flora and fauna and also on the livelihood of the small rice farmers. There were reports that the illegal blocking of watercourses endangered the manatee, salt-water intrusion resulted from the illegal widening and deepening of watercourses, and agricultural chemicals damaged fauna (Ramsar, 1996).

The conflict could be seen clearly in 1989, when Jabar, another large-scale rice farmer, bulldozed 40 hectares of Palm swamp forest. He had a forest offence matter pending and said that the Permanent Secretary in the Ministry of Agriculture gave him permission to be in the swamp (Wildlife Section, 1993). The Forestry Officers had no authority to act against him under the State Lands Act. However in this same year, 1989, the Bush Bush Wildlife Sanctuary was declared a Prohibited Area under the Forests Act on September 27th 1989. Entry to the area was regulated by permit from the Directory of Forestry with stipulated conditions. However restricting access to this sanctuary was constrained by the limited funds given to the Wildlife Section for game wardens in 1991.

Funds were provided for another study on rice production however. In 1991 the Agristudio Reconnaissance study for the extension of the Plum Mitan Scheme, Draft Final Report, was produced. One year later, in 1992, 14 applications for 1,045 acres in Nariva Swamp were made in 1 month. The State Lands Division of Ministry of Agriculture was accepting applications for State Lands within the Plum Mitan area. However squatters were then taking land in the Bush Bush Wildlife Sanctuary, Ortoire-Nariva Windbelt Reserve and proposed National Parks area. The Minister of Agriculture advised that no action could be taken against the squatters in the Bush Bush wildlife sanctuary because the boundaries were not clear.

The squatters were not the only ones entering the Nariva Swamp. In 1993 fifteen permits were given to enter Bush Bush Wildlife Sanctuary. The Trinidad and Tobago Field Naturalists Club undertook a research project on the status of the manatee in Nariva Swamp with the assistance of the Wildlife Section.
The San Juan Rotary Club collaborated on the conservation of the manatee in the Nariva Swamp, Manzanilla. The Wildlife Section was still starved of funds but Thomas Peake and Co. Ltd., donated $2,000.00 for gasoline and oil towards patrols for the Nariva Swamp (Annual Report of the Forestry Division, 1993). However inadequate vehicular transport hampered progress and widespread illegal activity continued in the Bush Bush Wildlife Sanctuary, and as such, work by the Wildlife Section was severely curtailed.

Nariva Swamp has been a legal entity since 1968. Its legal status in Trinidad was insufficient to preserve its ecological status. Active lobbying and effort was expended to give the Swamp the status of an internationally recognised entity and therefore remove it from solely national political decisions. International recognition came in 1992, when Trinidad and Tobago designated Nariva Swamp for the List of Wetlands of International Importance maintained under the Ramsar Convention. The Nariva Swamp was designated as a Wetland of International Importance (especially as a waterfowl habitat) under the Ramsar convention on 21 April 1993. Concerned officials of the Ministry of Agriculture lobbied for this international status to protect the Swamp from local political concerns and to make it easier to access international funding. Instruments were laid on December 21, 1992 with respect to the declaration of the Nariva Swamp as a Ramsar site. The total area of the Ramsar site is 6,234 hectares, which is the same area as the Nariva Swamp Prohibited Area and proposed National Park (CFCA, 1997).

The Nariva Swamp was included on the Montreux Record in 1993 in Kushiro, Japan (CFCA, 1997). This is a register of Ramsar sites where changes in ecological character have occurred, are occurring, or are likely to occur as a result of technological developments, pollution or other human interference. Ms. Molly Gaskin, and Ms. Karilyn Shephard of the Pointe á Pierre Wildfowl Trust, and Ms. Nadra Nathai-Gyan, of the Wildlife Section, Forestry Division, and Dr. Carol James, at the time with the UNDP-GEF, were present at this meeting.

The entire Nariva Swamp was declared a prohibited area under Section 2 of the Forests Act, Chapter 66:01. In May 1993 the Forestry Division accomplished the following:
ii. Boundaries within Nariva Swamp were identified - the Sanctuary and Proposed National Park.
111. Habitat evaluations in the squatted areas of Bush Bush Wildlife Sanctuary were done.
iv. Two comprehensive reports were written on the extent of squatting and its consequences to the environment of Nariva Swamp, and submitted to the Ministry of Agriculture, Land and Marine Resources.

In May 1993, the Ministry of Agriculture, Land and Marine Resources announced plans to evict all large rice farmers from Nariva Swamp and make it into a National Park.

On July 28th 1993, Justice Anthony Lucky ruled that the wildlife, flora and fauna in the Nariva Swamp must be protected in the public interest. Attorney Ramesh Lawrence Maharaj had claimed before Justice Anthony Lucky in the court case that the Jabars could be considered as squatters or persons in possession of lands with knowledge that he or she will be given the lands. Parbatie and Goolcharan Jabar, two of the large illegal rice farmers appealed against the Justice Lucky decision and conservatory order. Appeal Court Judge, Mme Justice Permanand, dismissed the Jabars' appeal on September 23, 1993. In February 1995, the Land and Surveys Division served 150 quit notices on farmers. Very few farmers left.

In 1994 a visit from a technical officer of the Ramsar Bureau, and the inception of the Monitoring Procedure for Nariva Swamp was made. The Forestry Division continued the eviction of squatters in Nariva Swamp and reported the blossoming of the project on the conservation of the West Indian manatee, and stimulated public interest for their successful involvement in this effort. Permits to enter Bush Bush Wildlife Sanctuary / Nariva Swamp Protected Area numbered 283 (Annual Report of the Forestry Division, 1994). In 1994 Thomas Peake and Co. Ltd.,. donated $4000.00 for gasoline and oil towards patrols for the Nariva Swamp (Annual Report of the Forestry Division, 1994).

In 1994, close collaboration was undertaken with the Ramsar Bureau with the visit of their technical officer for the Neotropical Region in October, Dr. Montserrat Carbonnel, and a specific objective of the visit being to hold preliminary discussions regarding the implementation of the Monitoring Procedure at the Nariva Swamp Ramsar site. The Scientific and Technical Review Panel of the Bureau deemed the Nariva site to be one of their five (5) priority projects for 1994, and field assessments were scheduled for March 1995. Dr. Carbonnel also made visits to other wetlands in Trinidad, and she recommended that applications for inclusion of some of these on the Ramsar list be made. It was suggested that application should be made to Ramsar's Wetland Conservation Fund to facilitate the necessary collection of data on these sites, and it was expected that this would be done in 1995. IUCN made offers of assistance for Nariva Swamp (Annual Report of the Forestry Division, 1994).

Despite the court case, rice farmers continued to occupy the Swamp and in 1995, staff of the Division of Lands and Surveys served 160 quit notices to illegal farmers (CFCA, 1997). The Ramsar team was also present in the Swamp and in April/May 1995, a Monitoring Procedure or Management Guidelines Procedure was carried out by a three-person team. The team comprised of one consultant from the Ramsar Bureau and two specialists in social and community aspects and wetland restoration (CFCA, 1997).

In July 1996, Ms. Molly Gaskin presented a petition of 12,000+ signatures to the government demanding that the illegal rice farming taking place in the Swamp had to stop. Despite the legal decision and quit notices being served, the illegal farming continued until November 1996. In October 1996, the farmers were finally forced to leave the Swamp.

The Government of Trinidad and Tobago through the Ministry of Agriculture, Lands and Marine Resources (MALMR) contracted the Institute of Marine Affairs (IMA) to conduct an environmental impact assessment (EIA) of activities within the

Nariva Swamp area, particularly the area known as Block B. The EIA was officially launched on September 5, 1997 (IMA, 1997). In addition to the EIA, a management plan for the Nariva Swamp was to be prepared together with a monitoring plan to monitor the impacts of the recommended activities of the management plan. The EIA consisted of 10 components:

i. Wetlands ecology, ii. Aquatic fauna, iii. Geology, soils and hydrology, iv. Machinery and roads, v. Water and soil quality, vi. Rice agronomy, vii. Socio-economics, viii. Economics, ix. Legislature control, x. Public education.

The environmental impact assessment (EIA) of activities within Block B began on August 25th, 1997. Data was collected from September 1997 to May 1998 on all aspects of the environment of Nariva Swamp; the impacts of large-scale rice farming in Block B were identified, and mitigatory recommendations were provided. Impacts were identified for three phases; namely (i) site modification (ii) agricultural operations and (iii) post-rice farming.

Governance

Governance represents a method or system that provides the mechanism through which island sustainable development could be attained. The reorientation of government to governance typically means using public resources for the functions that only government can provide while encouraging a greater role for the private sector and civil society (Hardjoeno et al., 1996). Governance has three dimensions: the political dimension includes the way in which state affairs are administered and regulated (laws), the technical includes the natural and human resource capacities, while the ability to accomplish the task (e.g. managerial capacity) represents the institutional dimension. Good governance includes systemic, political and administrative levels. A sound definition of governance must also include the history, practice and theory of the state as an agent in the development process (Leftwich, 1994).

According to the ISLE concept paper on Governance: it is the culture of a society that informs its behaviour and perceptions. Culture should therefore be an integral component of political and economic development and there are links between culture and governance, which is the way in which stakeholders in an institution, government, community, business or family live their power, rights and responsibilities. Any system of governance rests on a world-view ---- a set of assumptions and values that determines how power, rights and responsibilities are distributed and expressed; the stance that the self takes to the total environmental as expressed through its behaviour, ideas, body and feelings and inspirations (Hardjoeno et al., 1996). This has implications for Trinidad and Tobago when considering the culture of rice production, and the attitudes to development and the environment inherited from colonial times. This attitude is reflected in the article by Siurua (2006) who writes that:

> " If many of the biggest drivers as well as historical beneficiaries of biodiversity loss are located in Northern societies, why should developing countries now make sacrifices and "stop developing" in order to compensate for the destruction wrought largely by others, especially if the affluent societies are often not prepared to live as they preach."

The culture of the society is also to be overly conscious of how the outside world views Trinidad and Tobago and to be uncritically receptive to external policies that have specific gendered impacts.

Gender analysis

A definition of gender analysis as used in relation this study of governance issues of the Nariva Swamp is in order. Cornwall (1998) documents an example of African trainees who were told that they had conducted a gender-analysis exercise in their village wrongly because their diagrams revealed the hardships faced by adolescent men, who were caught between gerontocracy and a gendered division of labour. This analysis may also be described as "wrong" because it focuses equally on men (their positions, views and reactions) and women, and includes men's perceptions on gender issues. It also includes references to women who were seen to behave in 'patriarchal' ways. The inclusion of the male perspective is based on the insights of Cornwall (1998) who claims that too often 'gender' is taken to mean 'women' and something women should be concerned about while 'men' become the problem. This 'women-only' approach to gender can result in excluding men who would be interested in bringing about change, while it affronts those men who retain their patriarchal tendencies. The end result is that 'gender' becomes a battleground on which other struggles are waged (Cornwall, 1998).

The World Bank Participation Sourcebook, Appendix I: Methods and Tools suggests that the concept of gender analysis began from the need to mainstream women's interests while at the same time conceding that women could not be treated as a homogeneous group. It was realised that women's needs were better understood when viewed in relation to men's needs and roles and to their social, cultural, political, and economic context. Gender analysis thus takes into account women's roles in production, reproduction, and management of community and other activities. Changes in one of these roles may produce beneficial or detrimental effects in others. Data collected for gender analysis should be organised to highlight key gender problems, underlying causes of problems for men and women, and the relationship between problems and causes. The FAO's Socioeconomic and Gender Analysis package (SEAGA)[1] looks at how development policies and programmes have differential impacts on people in a society, based on socioeconomic patterns and structures (including gender relations) in that society. Some terms from the SEAGA package will be used in the analysis.

Gender Analysis Framework

Five major categories of information comprise gender analysis:
1. Practical and Strategic gender needs assessment
2. Activities profile
3. Resources, access, and control profile
4. Intra and inter-household benefits and incentives analysis
5. Institutional constraints and opportunities.

These categories of analysis were developed to address women's needs and were not applied to this governance and policy analysis of the issues surrounding the use of the Nariva Swamp. At the ISLE Gender Steering Committee meeting held in Halifax (11 -12 January, 1999) eight theoretical constructs of gender were identified:

1. access to and control of resources and benefits;
2. control of decision making;
3. productive and reproductive labour;
4. social and capital networks;
5. power, resistance and negotiation;
6. P/politics and collective action;

---

[1] SEAGA, contact: SEAGA/SDWW, Food and Agriculture Organization of the United Nations, Viale delle Terme di Caracalla, 00100 Rome, Italy. E-mail: SEAGA@fao.org

7. indigenous knowledge and discourse;
8. culture, ideologies, values and behaviours.

The most relevant of these theoretical constructs of gender are incorporated into the analysis e.g. social and capital networks, politics and collective action, culture, ideologies, values and behaviours. For example gender based differences in access to resources predict how different members of households, groups, and societies will participate in and be affected by planned development interventions is appropriate to this study. Also useful is a focus on understanding and documenting the differences in gender roles, activities, needs, and opportunities in the Nariva context. Other issues are how intermediate level institutions link macro-policy to households, the rules and practices through which institutions control the distribution of resources and the way that they reproduce gender disadvantages. Also relevant is gender bias within institutions, and the work values and work practices through which gender and social inequalities are reproduced (UNDP, 2000). The Gender analysis also highlights the different roles and learned behaviour of men and women based on gender attributes. These vary across cultures, class, ethnicity, income, education, and time.

Gendered analysis of the development context

Environmental issues often become multiple and interconnected sites of struggle. This is especially the case in Trinidad and Tobago where different groups have different visions of society, and differing access to resources and to power. These struggles are played out according to gender, race, class and ethnicity, variously connected in a complex political-economic situation. Issues pertaining to the environment are inherently political and decisions about the environment are not politically neutral.

Gender is a pivotal organising principle around which social, cultural and economic processes are structured. Gender shapes social and economic institutions from the household level to the macroeconomic, legal and political levels (FAO-SEAGA). All development interventions take place against a specific local background that includes patterns and linkages among socio-cultural, political, environmental, economic, demographic, institutional issues and socio-economic patterns (FAO-SEAGA). Macro-level policymakers are in general concerned with economic growth and modernisation and the welfare of populations.

The discourse2 and doxa of food self sufficiency

Doxa according to Bourdieu is that which is accepted as natural and self evident, beyond discourse or argumentation - rather than being actively contested and negotiated. For example the idea that unfettered markets are the key to economic efficiency and growth (FAO-SEAGA). This male-derived doxa has shaped all economic policies in the last few decades. Food self sufficiency and the legitimacy of large scale mechanised production can be seen as a doxa or perhaps an ideology - where ideology is a set of beliefs, a viewpoint that legitimises a particular kind of arrangement and makes it natural and morally acceptable. An ideology is a dominant value system, which permeates all spheres of life and is accepted by all, even those who are victimised by it (ISLE Gender Steering Committee meeting, 1999).

The Doxa of food self-sufficiency was enshrined in post-Independence policy in the Draft Second Five - Year Plan 1964 - 1968. National Planning Commission: Dr. Eric Williams, Mr. Arthur, N. Robinson, Mr. John O'Halloran, Mr. Robert Wallace, Mr. Lionel Robinson, Mr. Louis Alan Reece, Mr. Jack Harewood, Mrs. Patricia Robinson, Mr. David Weintraub and Mr. William Demas:

"The food import bill is not only high but growing and is now in the vicinity of the sum of $70 million per annum. A dominant objective of policy must therefore be to reduce the share of imports in total food consumption in order to achieve a greater degree of self-sufficiency and to protect the balance of payments. Rice constitutes a large part of the diet of most of the population. While annual per capita consumption has risen from approximately 86 pounds in 1955 to about 158 pounds in the 1960s. Local production had declined from 12,000 tons in 1952 to 10,000 tons in 1961. The contribution of local production to total supply has declined to 30 per cent. Rice is grown as a subsistence or subsidiary crop. Since 1952 the acreage under rice has declined from 18,000 acres to 15,000 acres in 1961. Land has been switched to the more profitable eddoes and sugar, the latter due to the expectation of a good quota on the American market.

---

[2] Discourse is a body of knowledge; the arena in which knowledge and power are fused. Those in power determine what is counted as knowledge (ISLE Gender Steering Committee meeting, 1999). Discourses are historically, socially, and institutionally specific structures of statements, terms, categories, and beliefs. As texts, they assert truths and claims for authority and legitimisation (ISLE Gender Steering Committee meeting, 1999).

Price-wise local growers cannot compete with British Guyana.

As far as quality is concerned, Trinidad rice is not in the forefront. Greater rice production locally would call for substantial capital investment for reclamation of swamp areas, for modernisation of the industry by the provision of drying and milling facilities, and for some degree of mechanisation and irrigation. The question therefore, resolves itself into whether the use of more land and capital for the purpose of rice cultivation would constitute the best use of these resources when it is considered that there are other sectors in agriculture where returns are likely to be greater. Thus the value of alternative production foregone by producing the crop must be closely considered before the adoption of any schemes designed to promote self-sufficiency over the next five years, especially when there are good prospects of purchasing large amounts of rice at cheap prices from several sources.

To admit this however is not to ignore the possibilities of encouraging the expansion of rice production in specific areas, particularly through the undertaking of limited drainage works and also perhaps through the provision of funds for the establishment of a rice-mill in the County of Caroni as one of the Agricultural Development Board projects. Under the sub-project; Land settlement and use of marginal areas, one major project, the Oropouche Drainage Scheme, should lead to increased production on a considerable acreage in the South. Attention is also being given to the Nariva Swamp area in an effort to ascertain its potential for development."

The policies did have an impact on rice production. Paddy production increased dramatically from 0.3 M kg in 1983 to 17.4 M kg in 1991. Both milk and rice benefited from direct government subsidies in the form of price supports. In 1990, the Producer Subsidy Equivalents (PSEs) for rice was 85% (MALMR, 1983: 10). [Milk increased from 8M litres in 1982 to 11.0 M litres in 1991. PSE of 65%].

The PSE is the measure of protection in the form of subsidy to maintain equal levels of farm income in the absence of other interventions (MALMR, 1983). The policies brought about increases in production levels of some commodities, however the self-sufficiency ratio is low and the situation is compounded by diminishing self-reliance as foreign exchange earnings from agricultural exports continue to decline (MALMR, 1983:15). In addition, the ratio of imports to demand requirements is relatively high even for basic commodities.

In 1992 the estimated figures were:

Category	percentage
Dairy and dairy products	90%
Rice	75%
Beef and veal	80%
Livestock feed ingredients	95%
Edible oil	75%
Fish and fish products	60%

Once a macro-economic policy like the Draft Second Five - Year Plan 1964 - 1968 above is in place it becomes part of the environment and overall conditions that shape a country's economic development and determines allocation of resources (FAO-SEAGA) (for example the provision of resources for rural roads in rice producing areas and the lack of funding for game wardens). The prevailing policy can also become part of the prevailing technocratic thinking. Economic and agricultural planners did not question the doxa of food self sufficiency:

" $4 million is not an unreasonable sum to subsidise food self sufficiency, but that argument breaks down if the local rice was pet rice, that would blow a big hole in the self sufficiency argument. We have the problem that we produce what we do not consume and consume what we do not produce. This is the worst of all possible worlds...to produce subsidised rice and feed it to dogs and then import rice for people. If you check and see no reduction in imports then they cannot say they were satisfying local demand."

However an Agricultural consultant was sceptical about Agricultural Planning in general:

"The planners put things up, then they find the justification after. When did they start to pay the subsidy to Jai Ramkissoon? If you check you will see that it was under Brinsley Samaroo. Jabar[3] went in under him. The agricultural statistics are easier to keep for rice. How much eddoes is

---

[3] One of the first large scale rice farmer/squatters to enter the swamp.

produced and imported? Those figures are not kept so easily. What comes through the CARICOM jetty? No one keeps those records. Records of rice go through customs, so it is easy to get those figures. We probably eat more ground provisions in combination than rice, but there is no system to collect that information. For rice we have to import seeds and machinery."

It is unclear whether ground provisions are considered "women's crops" and are marginalised because of this; or whether rice production produces more prestige for male farmers and agricultural planners because it is easier than ground provisions to grow on a large-scale and in a highly mechanised manner. Mechanised agriculture was grudgingly recognised by interviewees as a "man thing." This argument is developed in the section on Gender and Development. Rice is visible in the statistics and thus fits into the economic framework. Rice fits better than ground provisions into the dominant and male biased thinking that unfettered markets are the key to economic efficiency and growth (FAO-SEAGA). Ground provisions are brought into Trinidad by women traders from other Caribbean islands, whereas rice is dealt with at a macro level, for example the famous two shipments of rice from India that went astray were organised at the very top by male Ministers, Embassy officials and male members of the National Flour Mills. Rice is normally imported from the USA. This is a classic example of women remaining invisible in macro-level statistics.

Markets never function without policy intervention to lay ground rules (FAO-SEAGA). Markets are also increasingly subject to policy to make them freer, global, to revitalise them and extend them into peripheral sections of the economy (FAO-SEAGA). Therefore the policy decision to focus on rice rather than create policies and institutional support to facilitate the entry of women into markets either through their roles as small scale importers or as local providers of ground provision could be considered a gendered decision.

The Social and capital networks linking politicians and the Swamp

The popular view is that environmental degradation is poverty driven. There are limitations to this view; environmentally damaging behaviour also results from gender interests and ideologies (Jackson, 1993). Certain women can strike 'bargains with patriarchy' which link their interests to those of certain men rather than with women (Cornwall, 1998). This means that the processes of negotiation, contestation and collaboration between men and women need to be taken into account. Women and men in similar situations need not have common interests, so their social networks have to be taken into account.

Social and capital networks, politics and collective action, culture, ideologies, values and behaviours are part of gender analysis. For example gender based differences in access to resources to predict how different members of households, groups, and societies will participate in and be affected by planned development interventions.

Social capital was one component of the livelihood theoretical domain identified as useful of gender analysis at the ISLE Gender Steering Committee held in Halifax (11 -12 January, 1999). The livelihood domain also included access to and control over resources, benefits and decision-making.
Social capital refers to the ways in which exchange networks are mobilised to allow people to gain access to various resources necessary to their survival (ISLE Gender Steering Committee meeting, 1999). Social capital networks are usually gendered in that there may be complementary and or contradictory practices between the social capital practices of men and women, even within the same households. Many women use social capital networks to open up livelihood possibilities that are critical to their contributions to household livelihood. Men may use social capital networks in more vertical ways, for example to access the market for things in accordance with the conventions of local gender ideologies (for example, regarding men's breadwinner ideals) (ISLE Gender Steering Committee meeting, 1999).

The National Wetlands Committee (WLCC) was one important social network involved in the management of the Nariva Swamp. The Government eventually appointed this Wetlands Committee to make policy for wetlands when Ramsar was signed. Guptee Lutchmedial was appointed to the Wetlands Committee as a member of the San Juan Rotary Club. Molly Gaskin was appointed as the representative of the

Pointe à Pierre Wildfowl Trust and Sylvia Sylvia Kacal as a Non-Government person, not as a member of the Caribbean Forest Conservation Association. These three were appointed in the first round of this committee. The Wetlands Committee worked on policy and a strategic plan. This network was formed as a result of the Ramsar signing and did not arise from any Government commitment to Environmental policy. This WLCC network provided a point to mobilise so that the Wildlife Section could gain access to international resources they considered necessary for the survival of the Nariva Swamp. The approach to Ramsar was discussed for many years within the Forestry Division because:

> "we thought it would bring a more rational approach to the management of the Swamp. We thought the Government would be more likely to pay attention to international obligations as they did for CITES."

The approach to Ramsar was considered necessary because:

> "there was conflict for resources within the Ministry. No effort was made to manage the conflict. Tacit approval was given to the rice farmers; their actions were not prevented. The Thelen and Faizool draft policy for national parks was approved in principle. 61 National parks was considered too many, but Bush Bush was one."

It seems that even though the National Parks policy was approved in principle this was not enough to stop the rice farmers, or those in the Ministry of Agriculture who supported rice production in the Swamp. The conflicts surrounding the Nariva Swamp can be linked to the tendency of each interest group to see the issue through one set of eyes or one set of interests. For example in 1992, the State Lands Division of the Ministry of Agriculture was accepting applications for State Lands within the Plum Mitan area, which led to the land grabbing situation. This action of the State Lands Division was described as a:

> "blinkered management approach, a strongly sectoral management approach. The State Lands Division considered it to be their jurisdiction and their mandate to give out lands. It could be that the Parliamentary Secretary for the area approached the Division and asked for lands to be given to his constituents."

To transform natural goods and services into resources, people apply other types of capital to natural capital. People use social capital to mobilise social relationships, in accordance with cultural norms, to secure access to things which they normally could not afford, or to which they would have no access (ISLE Gender Steering Committee meeting, 1999). For example the San Juan Rotary Club had a 'save the manatee' project together with Wildlife, they not only took all the credit, but also restricted access to people they knew:

> "Guptee is running it personally for friends and family but originally it was a good project."

In the Nariva rice farming situation the things exchanged through the social capital network were access to free land, water, village labour, mechanised technologies, subsidies for rice production, a refurbished mill and access to government policy and plans. In this case the Social capital network was based on the common religion and ethnic community. Since the exchanges cross class lines in that Government Ministers were involved and the large farmers were of an unequal social position, this was vertical social capital. The social capital was based perhaps upon reciprocity, but certainly on obligation and dependency. The rules and practices through which the Ministry controlled the distribution of resources were therefore informal. The only woman farmer mentioned in the interviews was Theresa Akaloo; an Afro-Trinidadian married to one of the large rice farmers. From the interviews conducted it seems that the PNM[4]-Muslim Indo-Trinidadian Minister spoke only to Theresa's husband Zahir; but the NAR[5]-Afro-Trinidadian Minister who succeeded him knew Theresa (Ashick was another member of the family involved). This Minister claimed that:

> "Theresa Akaloo was better than the others. Back in 1987/88, when people started expanding, she attempted to proceed along a responsible path. She always discussed with the Ministry what she was doing, used proper management, and told us what was taking place."

The first comment made by the PNM-Muslim Minister of Agriculture in his interview was that the large rice farmers were Muslims. There were also villagers who claimed that the large rice farmers gained access to rice land because [this Minister] made a cook in the swamp, and gave them permission."

As stated by a former Minister of Agriculture, the larger farmers were well

---

[4] People's National Movement one of the original political parties.

[5] National Alliance for Reconstruction, a recently formed political party, formed from members of previous parties.

heeled politically or economically meaning that they had access to a social network. A previous Agriculture Minister confirmed this:

"The Bearded Akaloo wanted to do a project in the rice area. Ministers don't give out land, but I offered to see what I could do, and he applied for 200 acres. The Ministry of Agriculture offered 100 acres within the area abandoned within Plum Mitan. The Rice mill was refurbished in my time and the 89 cents subsidy was given in my time. Guyana and Suriname rice was cheaper but it was a deliberate policy to get more local rice, to support local people and the big Akaloos. What they did since then I don't know. The only person I dealt with was Zahir Akaloo, he had a wonderful plan, it benefited the Ministry, he was a leader in field of rice cultivation; Plum Mitan developed under him."

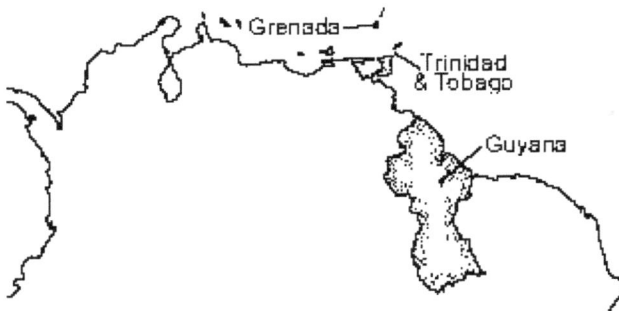

Fig 5. Comparative sizes of Trinidad and Guyana

A second Agriculture Minister also spoke of the established linkages between himself and the large farmers:

"I was confident that the large farmers could get through because they had excellent quality rice. I said they should apply for land and I would go with the project to Cabinet. I said they would all get pieces of land, 100 to 200 acres since there was limited space. I met the large farmers frequently and I had a good, informal relationship with them. They were a whole set of Muslim fellows. I was pleased with the initiative they had shown; I couldn't throw them out. "

Can the importance put on rice by national governments as opposed to other crops be due to the power, authority and technical competence of the élites who have favoured intensive agriculture, including rice production? Can the large-scale Muslim rice farmers been considered a political elite? The interview below is reproduced to show what Bourdieu (1977) calls 'officialising strategies'. This means that the particular interests of key sectors of the community become identified with the general interest. So the egoistic, personal and particular interests of rice farmers are represented as the disinterested, collective, publicly avowable, legitimate need for national food self sufficiency. In the interview statements of the Prime Minister are quoted as endorsements and used to 'officialise' the rice farmers' private interests. The interview was also seen as an opportunity to document the rice farmers' position.

The interviewee, Theresa Akaloo, was seen as a major player by most of the people interviewed. She was not only the wife of a large-scale rice farmer, but also the President of the Rice Growers Association. Interviewees volunteered the information that Theresa Akaloo was honest and straightforward and they seemed to admire her in her own right. In the July-August period of 1996 Theresa was supposed to present a paper at a Conference in Guyana called *50 Years of Rice*, but became caught up in the escalating conflict over the Nariva Swamp. She claimed to be the only prominent woman in the TIRGA. The links to this intermediate level institution helped the large-scale rice farmers' link agricultural macro-policy to their household income. It seems that she was accepted as a female leader based on her personality and ability and her non-Indian race was mentioned, but not dwelt on. Judging from the interview with her and two other farmers whatever concern she had about the environment came a distant second to the drive to maximise rice production:

"Zahir was in Block A, but Ministry officers stopped him, and told him to go into Block B which was under consideration by the Ministry for rice production. Plum Mitan was one of the major areas of expanded cultivation planned for rice production in the Draft Public Sector Investment Programme laid in Parliament by Planning and Mobilisation Minister Winston Dookeran in 1988. The other wetland areas mentioned were Caroni and Oropouche. Technical and economic feasibility studies were commissioned to assess whether these areas could be utilised to increase self-sufficiency from 10% to the 40 million pounds of rice consumed annually. It took us years to produce profitably on 1400 acres. We are comfortable not wealthy. The whole Swamp is 65,000 acres. If boats from the small islands don't come in we would starve. The Japanese consultant[6] surprised by the technology we had in Swamp in 1991. The

---

[6] Mr. Sousuke Haga, a Japanese International Corporation Agency (JICA) rice seed expert was on assignment to the Trinidad and Tobago government in October 1987.

Express of March 16th 1996 has an article on the Food deficit. Prime Minister Panday expressed concerned about our lack of food security. We have a right to earn a livelihood by growing food, peacefully and in harmony with the nation. Farmers should be recognised as people and earn respect and should be honoured for producing food. Without farmers there would be no food and no rice. Food comes first. There are floods in Guyana now, which will lead to a grain shortage. The amount of rice being planted here is important and must support the local industry. The small farmers who speak out against us want to go back to ganja. We have to be large scale to see profits. Hand harvesting is not profitable. Gaskin is looking for international fame that is why she is against us. Our status in the Swamp is not legal, but to call us illegal farmers doesn't sound good. "

This interview was given before at a critical stage in the Nariva crisis and Theresa's leadership abilities are seen clearly. She was using the opportunity to demonstrate her possession of the 'capital of authority' necessary to impose a definition of a situation, in a crisis moment when the nation's collective judgement on the best use for the Nariva Swamp wavered. Theresa is also placing the issue within the "discourse[7]" of food security.

The social capital networks linked to rice farming provided certain farmers with social safety nets, since according to one of the interviewees one large scale rice farmer (and perhaps others) used the rice subsidy to pay off poultry production debts:

"Ramroop Jabar was a poultry farmer from Las Lomas. He had a contract with Cannings but he was not making money because of the pilfering going on at his place. He went on his own but he did worse, he had no management skills. I met him by the rum shop in Curepe. He told me that he paid off his poultry debts with the rice subsidy. From 1982 - 1985, Jabar was planting a little rice by his home."

This particular social capital exchange network between Agriculture Ministers and rice farmers allowed the large-scale rice farmers access to the natural resource base (free land and water) in Nariva Swamp, which was far from their home locality of Cunupia and Las Lomas. Social capital networks became a vehicle for negative use patterns. Privatisation and mechanised agriculture resulted in greater demands on the

---

7

natural resource in order to sell rice in the market place. Environmentalists saw this large-scale rice production as rapidly becoming unsustainable. One Minister of Agriculture hints at this unsustainability by referring to the project to introduce fresh water into the Oropouche Swamp. This Swamp and the Swamp at Fishing Pond had been damaged by saltwater intrusion linked to rice production. Rice farmers caused other damage like pesticide contamination. Some environmentalists and Wildlife Officials claimed that the same rice farmers who damaged Fishing Pond and South Oropouche then moved into Nariva (Wildlife Section, 1993). The saltwater intrusion is officially documented in internal Ministry of Agriculture documents…

"Indications are that more than 1000 acres of rice lands have had to be abandoned in this area. Further, it has been reported that the gradual increase in the salinity of soils in the Caroni and Fishing Pond areas, have also rendered sizeable areas of land (previously under rice) unsuitable for rice cultivation " (Planning Associates, 1981).

Below an interview extract from another Minister of Agriculture demonstrates the patron-client relationship, his respect for the technological approach of the large-scale farmers, and his loss of control over the actions of the large-scale farmers:

"I tried to encourage the rice farmers to set up a co-op to ensure that they got Government help. The Government had tractors; I could have got them to work for a month to clear the land. I could have pushed as the Minister for better roads and drainage. I could have settled 10 large farmers with 100 acres each. One scheme was to give out Block C with 5-acre plots. Other Blocks could have been brought in at a later stage. A regularisation of those that were there could have taken place. But they decided to move into Blocks, they were opening it up for themselves. They built a huge shed over the main road into the Swamp. Molly Gaskin was surrounded and abused 'She is humbugging we living'. It was a situation of lawlessness."

The Express also reported on this incident (Tue Aug 18, 1998 pg 3. Nariva rice rage – farmers block access to swamp). The Ministries of Agriculture and Works accompanied by police went in to refill the channels. The farmers parked a harvester across a bridge into the swamp that they had built. They claimed that Minister of Agriculture Dr. Reeza Mohammed had told them everything was all right two weeks before at a meeting in Princes Town.

For the rice farmers the social capital network allowed access to numerous goods and services, which increased their quality of daily life (ISLE Gender Steering Committee meeting, 1999). The social network is also apparent in that the then Minister claimed that squatters could be charged only after clear boundaries had been established for Bush Bush wildlife sanctuary, the Ortoire Nariva Windbelt Reserve and the proposed National park. Interviewees claimed that this was:

> "A red herring. The Minister is using the lack of boundaries to avoid the issue of rice farmer squatting."

The goods and services the rice farmers were able to assess were located outside of the formal market place, since the land use was informally sanctioned and only offered to a particular group of farmers. It is important to think of the importance individuals attach to social capital relative to that attached to environmental capital. This is because people might not want to give up social exchange networks even when the obligations and reciprocal exchanges they necessitate produce unsustainable livelihood practices.

Social exchange networks can also induce people to mobilise scarce resources in ways that seem wasteful or are essentially unaffordable (ISLE Gender Steering Committee meeting, 1999). In maintaining social capital networks in these ways, people are symbolically affirming the social relations they rely upon for survival (ISLE Gender Steering Committee meeting, 1999). In situations of environmental degradation these social networks may appear to people to be a more worthwhile "investment", than their environment. For example, when people use destructive fishing technologies and give away part of the catch rather than risk a smaller catch, which provides nothing to share (ISLE Gender Steering Committee meeting, 1999), and when rice farmers offer politicians:

> "Scotch and Rum…or to "cook up a manatee, monkey or goat."

Three Ministers of Agriculture tried to steer a middle course that would appease both the environmentalists and the rice farmers:

> "We had never taken the position that there should be no rice farming. Some responsible farming should go on but the irresponsibility going on must stop."

A former Minister of Agriculture touched on the conflict of interest involved in a State institution giving loans to the large-scale rice farmers to grow rice on land to which they had no legal tenure. This Minister claimed that the ADB staff approved the loans for a different area.

Gendered power relations: - how do women and men feel about the above practices?

The conflict over the Nariva swamp developed in part due to a conflict in values[8]. Interviewees felt that Trinidadians:

"Were not comfortable with open green spaces. Trinidadians think that the bush has to be tamed, the bush is hostile and dangerous and therefore it is doing a good thing to clean it away. Others like the green spaces but in a passive way, they are accustomed to it. Other people look at these green spaces as a basis for profit, they want a fete, housing, sporting arenas and a big profit. [These were considered to be] historical attitudes, or a colonial attitude to development."

The conflict was also seen in racial terms. During a debate in the House of Representatives on Friday 22nd January 1981, the Member for Tabaquite Mr. Nizam Mohammed challenged the Government on their attitude towards agriculture:

"This Government has always been accused of deliberately sabotaging agriculture, mainly because certain people in this country of a certain ethnic group are mainly involved in agriculture. This has been said for 25 years and I say this without any apology because none of them can deny that fact... We would have had a programme of land zoning to prevent prime agricultural land being converted to other purposes. We would not have allowed agricultural lands to remain idle. And then we would have undertaken a programme of swamp reclamation. Now they would say that they are doing this but for 10 to 15 years they have been doing that in the Nariva Swamp, telling the country that not only would Nariva be supplying Trinidad but we would have sufficient rice for export. You go up there and there are only two clearances for catching cascadura. Nothing has been done and millions have been spent year after year. We are glad for the

---

[8] The ISLE definition of values - a socially shared proposition which embodies a preference, choice or designation of rightness. Values are not susceptible to proof; earlier called "good" (ISLE Gender Steering Committee meeting, 1999).

people who get employment up there, but the point is, if there had been some objective, some proper planning at least the money would have been spent and we would have had some kind of positive results" (Hansard, 1982, pg. 376 and 384).

Interviewees echoed the view that certain ethnic groups were associated with rice production:

"You wouldn't find many governments saying we shouldn't produce as much rice as possible as long as it is economic. I guess it was not economic, but it was subsidised. I am not sure but it was probably cheaper to import the rice. Sugar is also uneconomic; we are selling it at a loss, less than the production cost. Rice has the same ethnic issues attached to it as sugar. There is a difference in that there are more private farmers involved in rice and less state involvement... In terms of policy it is political economy. The Indian community is part of the thing. The neglect of agriculture is seen to be a lack of support for the Indian population. The Indians were pushing flour milling as well. Government was not so crass as to neglect the Indian population, but not so transparent either, they gave concessions. Caroni is seen as a direct subsidy to the East Indian community. The local political dynamic is tied to the racial thing. It is the squatting thing all over again. "

An interviewee also commented on the 'political strategy or choice' of the Afro-Trinidadian wife of a large rice farmer (ethnic Indian and Muslim) as the spokesperson for the group of large rice farmers. Since she was qualified for the role it is difficult to judge whether this was also a political strategy.

However there were many objectors to what was taking place in the swamp. One interviewee claimed that:

" There are people who don't care how they make their money. Their culture says money is God. People who went into the Swamp did it because it was a money thing. The most scandalous part of the whole thing was that it was a state agency receiving this rice that was being grown on prohibited land, and the rice was of poor quality... It was interesting to watch those people from Cunupia, the spokespeople. The Muslims have a kind of expansionist approach, supported by thinly veiled criminal tactics. The Strong arm is the Muslimeen. They target certain things to develop and bring money into. Some industries are a good cash front for laundering; the banks can't track the money. The Nariva scenario could have been a land grab... Land is the basis for all wealth, value without putting out anything."

A lawyer interviewed in 1996 before the farmers left the Swamp, claimed that: "Someone could initiate a complaint, they could contact the Environmental Management Authority (EMA). The EMA should bring civil and criminal action. Both could be done together, private prosecution, malicious damage to property, civil action destruction of livelihood, damage, trespass and general damages. A system should be set up to take care of our natural heritage instead of individuals saying how they want State Lands to be used. EMA are watchdogs for our interests, it is their duty to act, they cannot ignore this situation. Responsible officials can be found personally liable, they did not prevent violation, they had knowledge of it, once it is drawn to their attention; therefore the ADB is potentially liable. Call the rice farmers land grabbers. Cite Justice Lucky's statements: borrowed our money, stole our land, they are behaving like bandits; they are behaving like brigands not farmers. Technically they are in contempt of court. Separate proceedings are needed to bring lay documentation, to bring the matter to court, establish burden of proof, beyond reasonable doubt, brought to the judges attention in proper form, for example...on such and such a date this occurred."

The women involved in the Wildlife Section were frustrated in their attempts to resolve the issue. The WLCC committee was called "just a talk shop", so that Molly Gaskin was called by a member of the Wildlife Section and asked to go to Nariva with Minister Keith Rowley when he was making an official visit. The Wildlife Section claimed that this was a last ditch effort to convince environmentalists about the issues that were being raised at the WLCC.

"Molly was appalled by the destruction and jumped to action. She embarked on public action, a strategy unavailable to public servants. She gave enormous assistance in the field and catapulted the Nariva issue into the spotlight."

MacGregor (2004) points out that in the past ecofeminists have ignored the emotions beyond caring ones, such as anger, outrage, and perhaps even selfishness that drive many women's engagement with environmental disputes and claims that more complex and multi-layered interpretations should be used.

The Wildlife Section also wrote correspondence to the Ministry trying to get the issue resolved. Another strategy was to collect the evidence needed for a court case to remove the large farmers. This evidence can be found in the Wildlife Section's Historical Issues Document. Additionally the Wildlife Section held a series of meetings with judges Stewart Best and Nolan Bereaux, to discuss this document and the potential case. Additionally it was claimed that the Forestry Division did not know where the boundaries of the Sanctuary were and needed to know in order to have a legal case:

> "There was a need to know how much the large farmers were encroaching on the sanctuary, and how much land they were occupying. The idea was to evict the large farmers from the Sanctuary not from Block B entirely. There was frustration on Forestry's part. We were talking about the issue before the farmers reached down to the Sanctuary, but they kept expanding and we had to make the boundaries. The situation was out of hand. We wanted the situation resolved. Even the Ministry's plans to redistribute the plots of forty hectares were thwarted. They were changing the whole water regime. The water doesn't stop at the boundary of the park; it was a Wild West situation. The swamp system also affects the park. In response to the boundaries established by the Forestry Division, large farmer Hosein took out the stakes at first. Eventually however the large farmers left the boundary marks and a line of trees grew up in the rice fields."

Gender and Development

The biggest threat to the Swamp came from large-scale rice farming. Is the choice to grow rice in the swamp a gendered one and is the push towards large-scale rice growing based on masculine notions of progressive agriculture? According to one interviewee:

> "The large rice farmers were operating at a completely different level. They were large scale and they had impressive machines. They were not the same small farmers, though they were also squatting. There would have been no drama if they had been small scale. It all came together. The farmers had been agitating for a long time for the Mill. National Flour Mills came in; all the pre-conditions were there, the large-scale production and milling. Rice

is a staple crop; it was easy to justify the large-scale farmers after the fact. Their backers could always tag on food self sufficiency."

The push towards progressive agriculture is revealed in the 1981 Report of Planning Associates, which claims that:
"It is imperative for the Ministry of Agriculture to urgently address the fundamental requirement for mechanisation wherever possible, and particularly on new lands planned to be brought under rice cultivation. The necessity for large contiguous tracts of land is a pre-requisite for effective mechanisation. Such a requirement appears to be in direct conflict with the Ministry's current strategy of segmentation into smallholdings. "

Gendered thinking is hidden behind such terms as "economies of scale" [which are] important when you are trying to control a watercourse, block a river and set up polders. It was claimed that:
"Even women should not want one-acre plots... Why stay in the subsistence mode? "

Another interviewee claimed that:
"If you say that men are more interested in large-scale mechanised farming you are making a leap of the mind. You are equating 1000 acres of rice with a phallus. But certainly mechanised agriculture is a man thing."

These two views were not selected as representative but as illustrations of range of the views on gender that exist. These views may indicate that mechanised or modernised forms of agriculture are seen as gender-neutral.

Gender and Forestry

Gender analysis looks at the rules and practices through which institutions control the distribution of resources and the way that they reproduce gender disadvantages. This section provides examples of the reinforcement of gender biases within institutions, and the work values and work practices through which gender and social inequalities are reproduced.
One of the ways that gender impacts on Forest policy is in the choice of species for reforestation. In many Third World countries woodlots of exotic species are planted which are suited to construction (a generally male responsibility) (Jackson, 1993). However in Trinidad gender and forestry were linked in terms of prestige.

Female officers revealed that there was a perception that Forestry was a male bastion. On the other hand National Parks and Wildlife was seen as a 'softer' area best left to women with Biology as opposed to Forestry degrees. Mainly the women employed in the Wildlife Section undertook advocacy in the Nariva Swamp issue. Perhaps their training in Biology gave them a more holistic view of the Swamp's value. Interviewees also expressed the view that male leadership in the Forestry Division was not as effective as it could have been. It was said that "troublemakers" were assigned to the Wildlife Section, and that the latest World Bank National Parks plan was not popular with Forestry, since male Forestry officers thought that the Plan would result in a loss of professional territory for them:

> "They didn't think that National Parks and Wildlife was as important as Forestry. Forestry was concerned about cutting trees, taming the environment... the Forestry Officers were not conservation minded. The Wildlife Section's budget was small, the chain of command was long, there were no substantive posts, they were managing large acreages and they needed more manpower."

Despite these realities changed circumstances were giving great status to Environmental issues. These changed opportunities meant that that the female staff of the Wildlife Section, who were seen as the "poor relatives" were getting professional opportunities, while Forestry officers were seeing the erosion of their male bastion. One view on the gendered work place politics is given below:

> "[Men are interested in] more opportunities, power, title, influence, all those things that testosterone likes to brew."

This view is reproduced because there were hints that the National Parks and Wildlife Section would be marginalised under the new Minister, based on the advice of the male head of the Forestry Division that the progress of work done under the section was not adequate.

Gender in the local context

As stated above gender analysis also highlights the different roles and learned behaviour of men and women based on gender attributes. Also relevant is gender bias within institutions, and the work values and work practices through which gender and social inequalities are reproduced. Gender analysis also highlights the different roles and learned behaviour of men and women based on gender attributes. These vary across cultures, class, ethnicity, income, education, and time. For example in one conflict between women Molly Gaskin[9] was pushed in the Swamp by one of the wives of one of the large-scale rice farmers who then tried to escape from retaliation by claiming that Muslim women could not be touched. MacGregor (2004) claims that the women who star in ecofeminist dramas are often engaged in processes of political and personal transformation, but this aspect has been neglected in ecofeminist texts except for Lee Quinby's "ecofeminism as a politics of resistance."

The roles of women in Trinidad is complicated by the perception that women have equal status, and this equality is deemed to be disadvantageous to young men as claimed by one interviewee[10]:

"I do not think that women Ministers are any different. Women do not alter the structure once they are in it; female capitalists are the same as male. Women say they want to join the army, they don't say stop war. The women leaders are not behaving any differently. I would be interested to see how many women middle managers there are in Trinidad. It is the young men who are in crisis."

It would seem in this case that the women mentioned had failed to live up to the expectation that due to their traditional roles and learned behaviour that they would bring something different to the workplace environment. However a Forestry Officer who didn't want to copy the autocratic and bureaucratic style of his senior colleagues copied one woman's leadership style. The idea that senior staff did not go into the field but sent junior staff was said to originate with male seniors but it was said that those female staff that observed it copied these ideas. This may mean that female staff followed what they considered to be the norm set by previous male leaders rather than bringing a women's-type of leadership into the workplace.

Another issue raised was that a female activist made the green issues emotional issues. A female consultant who prided herself on making objective choices and always being paid for her work raised this point, whereas two prominent female environmental activists prided themselves on doing volunteer work. Volunteer work is usually associated with women. There are new theories of the body and emotions that claim women can bring a new perspective to various issues since men are trained

[9] Key activist associated with the Wildlife Trust in Pointe á Pierre.
[10] Agricultural consultant.

to separate their bodies from their minds, whereas women aren't. Men have also charged prominent activists as being "emotional Gaskinites." There was another comment on emotions linked to the "stealing of credit" from the Wildlife Section by the San Juan Rotary Club, the quote was that "Wildlife was always getting itself hurt." A female environmental consultant also distanced herself professionally from the "emotional" label:

> "Molly queried why Nariva was not chosen as one of the three National Parks, it was in the top few but not in the top three. It was based on objective ranking with weightings not emotions. "

Locke (1999) claims that there is a need to question the validity of approaches that insist on the involvement of women, irrespective of their [women's] interest in the issues or their ability to articulate their views in a male arena. Gender struggles and environmental struggles are just as likely to be in conflict as to coincide according to Jackson (1993). The fact that more men are responsible for logging rainforests and are more likely to work in mining is not an indication that women are more environmentally friendly. Interviews conducted by Wahab (1997) clearly show the priorities of the swamp communities: 4 of the men and women interviewed said that any management plan for the swamp should share lands, with a minimum of 10 acres per family. One man from Brigand Hill wanted 100 acres. Wahab's interview with the Plum Mitan Women's Group reveals the sentiment that the large farmers opened their eyes to large-scale rice production. Not only did the large farmers harvest for some of the small farmers, the Women's Group claimed that if the large rice farmers were forced out 'the swamp gone again'. This implies that this Women's Group saw the impact of the large farmers on the Swamp as a good thing and that they had struck 'patriarchal bargains' that linked their interests to those of the large-scale male rice farmers. The Biche male interviewees and a Biche family also praised the large farmers for improving the access to fish by pumping out the water from their rice fields. Out of the more than 40 interviews, only one person, a woman from Kernahan, said that the Swamp was beautiful.

Gender and advocacy

According to Jackson (1993) we cannot use the involvement of women in 'environmental' protests as green credentials. However interviewees were of the opinion that more women in Trinidad than men were involved in advocacy and that Molly Gaskin's writings in the paper made the Nariva issue reach as far as it did. One interviewee claimed that:

> "Her writings influenced Minister of Agriculture Keith Rowley to take unpopular political decisions."

At the Kushiro conference, Carol James went as the Head of the Wildlife Section; Nadra Nathai-Gyan also went as part of the section. Molly Gaskin and Karilyn Shephard went as the NGO representatives. It was not a coincidence that only women went since "women with Biology degrees" were put into the Wildlife Section and "women activists and volunteers" were running the Pointe à Pierre Wildfowl Trust. According to the interviewees there are more women in the Environmental and Conservation groups. Some women started out in the Trinidad and Tobago Field Naturalists Club. The role of this Club was exploring the natural resources and disseminating information; despite longstanding debate on the usefulness of activism it is not an activist club. The activists left the Club and formed the CFCA. Sylvia Kacal was the first president of the CFCA, however the idea for its formation came from the Junior Minister of Environment at that time, Eden Shand. Advocacy at the policy level involved both genders:

> "When Ramsar was signed, they eventually appointed a Wetlands Committee to make policy and work on a strategic plan. Molly, Guptee and Sylvia Kacal were members. Prof. Bacon and Gerard Alleng from the IMA were the technical experts. Bacon was a tower of strength. Of the Ministry people, Potts went to study; Salandy didn't come. The Ramsar assessment pushed for squatter regularisation and an EIA. The Wetlands Committee pushed for the Ramsar site, it had to be done as a foundation for the future, and to push for a management plan."

The approach to shift the policy environment for Nariva Swamp away from local politics into the international arena was done to accomplish the following outcome: Nariva Swamp policy, regulations and plans would henceforth have to meet the international criteria set by the Ramsar Commission. In addition to approaching Ramsar coalition building also took place, e.g.

1. A large public outcry was created about the issue to force the hands of the Minister of Agriculture, this made the wetlands for rice policy less politically feasible than before;
2. Powerful organisations in Trinidad and Tobago linked together to create the issue as one of national importance and also tried to get the issue discussed in Parliament.

The approach to Ramsar was a deliberate strategy to provide an alternative to the prevailing anti-environmental thinking and to foster a new "discourse" that was more environmentally friendly. Textually mediated discourses are becoming new forms of social relations that transcend and organise local settings and bring about new sets of connections (ISLE Gender Steering Committee meeting, 1999). The elaboration of any discourse is embedded in conflict and power. Not all discourses carry the same weight; those that deviate from, or challenge, the prevailing system and its practices are likely to be marginal and dismissed as irrelevant or bad (ISLE Gender Steering Committee meeting, 1999). The conflict over which discourse would prevail, food security vs. environmental conservation, was played out in the Magistrate's courts:

> "Magistrate Kenny Persad talked about men who should be complimented for growing food instead of being charged for damage to 2 parrots and 4 monkeys, and a minimal fine of $43 was given to the large-scale farmers who bulldozed the swamp. All the time, the Swamp and the environment were not considered important. The Wildlife Section was asked why we were harassing little people. Magistrate Jurity talked about 2 birds in a cage versus agricultural development. There was also the claim that the laws were white men's laws. The police as well were not sympathetic, and wouldn't give the game wardens assistance because they said they had more important things to do and only had a few vehicles. On April 30, 1996 in the court matter vs. Jabar, Sukhoo, Jaimungal and Jaikaran at the Rio Claro District Court, the total fines were $5,100.00. Traditionally in Trinidad, decision makers and policy makers have looked on swamps as useless. The idea was to satisfy the needs of a growing population. How can we use the useless land?"

Advocacy also took place through enrolling the Caribbean Conservation Association who created "The Nariva Resolution" at the 32nd Annual General Meeting on Aug 28, 1998. They urged that any agriculture should be confined to Block A. They encouraged the government to approve the 1996 National Wetlands Policy and called upon the government to honour the Ramsar contract to refill the illegal channels in Block B. On Wednesday August 19th the Express printed a Krishna Maharaj photo with the caption "Nariva on the boil" of the large farmers enjoying a port of pelau during their stand off with the police over their return to the swamp. A large manned harvester is in the background.

Greenpeace was also part of the pressure strategy. Tom Clemens the Senior Campaigner of Greenpeace International (Washington) faxed another letter to Prime Minister Basdeo Panday copied to Honourable Dr. Reeza Mohammed, MP, Minister of Agriculture, Lands and Marine Resources, on September 2, 1998 urging the "Government to recognize the worth of the natural ecological characteristics of Nariva and to halt the threats to it." .. "we ask that your Government take all steps to ensure the safety and well-being of Molly Gaskin, whose work to protect Nariva is recognized by our organization as being exemplary."

The Vice President of the WWF Latin American and Caribbean Program, Dr. Twig Johnson, wrote a similar letter to both parties on Sept 4, 1998 recognising the need for small scale farming in Block A but "fearing that large scale rice farming will be incompatible with your nation's commitment to protect the ecological integrity of Nariva for future generations"… With the upcoming 7th Meeting of the Conference of the Contracting Parties to Ramsar in San Jose, Costa Rice in May of 1999, much greater attention will be focused on the Latin American and Caribbean Parties and their efforts to implement the Ramsar Convention."

A three page notice entitled *Big Rice Farmers Move In On Nariva Again*!! gave a summary of the NGO concerns about the situation regarding the refilling of the illegally dug channels in the Nariva and the big farmers attempts to stop this. The fourth page consisted of information from the November 1996 study "Nariva Swamp: An Exercise in Environmental Economics" (Keeler and Pemberton, 1996). A double-sided one-pager was circulated. On one side it was headlined 'Why you should help to save a national treasure, the Nariva wetlands. An overview. On the other side the title was Some of the negative impacts of large scale rice farming, Block B. The first paragraph:

"After a violent confrontation where an NGO, the Pointe à Pierre Wildfowl's Trust's Molly Gaskin was cuffed by an Akaloo wife in the presence of 2 Government Ministers, the Police and illegally squatting big rice farmers, and following upon a silent protest by NOG's at the Senate in November 1996, the Government of Trinidad and Tobago implemented the earlier Cabinet decision and moved the big rice farmers squatting in the Nariva Swamp, a RAMSAR site of international importance. Third paragraph: More than 22,000 people petitioned the Government to protect the Nariva Swamp and the livelihoods of the small farmers and fishermen, and called for the removal of the illegally squatting big rice farmers.

2nd side, first paragraph. 3 of the 5 families farming illegally in a big way, 1200 hectares, have benefited personally to the tune of $7 million per year in rice subsidy alone. Between 1986 – 1996 no income tax was paid, no land rent paid; did not pay for water. Soft loans were obtained from the Agricultural Development

Bank and other banks, inspite of not having tenure nor leases! 2nd side, sixth paragraph. These same big rice farmers squatting in Block B also damaged the Oropouche Swamp and Fishing Pond previously, leaving behind destruction valued at about $2 million.

Discourses are produced within particular epistemological and cultural conditions, which arise out of given historical situations like the Nariva conflict. Therefore a shift in ideological and material exigencies at certain historical conjunctures makes possible the elaboration of new and / or refashioned objects, concepts and methodologies. The approach to Ramsar and the designation of the swamp as a wetland of international importance produced the paradigm shift that the Wildlife Section needed.

The resulting environmental discourse however relies on the production of 'facts', like the EIA, in their own support. This process of producing facts transpires in the everyday practices of institutions. Whether due to the 'green credentials' of the Wildlife Section and the Pointe á Pierre Wildfowl Trust or to the external funding environment that has incorporated environmental concerns into its mandates, the Government's rhetoric (discourse) towards the Nariva Swamp has changed. This is clearly seen in the 1994 - 1996 White Paper on Agriculture. Page 3 of the document lists Sector Resources as Natural Resources, Agricultural Lands, Wetlands, Water Resources, Forest Resources and Fisheries Resources. Under the category Wetlands is the following paragraph:

> Quote 1: The major wetlands of ecological importance are located in Trinidad and include such areas as the Nariva Swamp (6,234 hectares); Caroni Swamp (5,611 hectares); South Oropouche Lagoon (5,642 hectares) and Fishing Pond (1,220 hectares). Mangrove forests make up a substantial proportion of most wetlands, except for manmade lakes and the inland savannahs, which include, Erin (40 hectares) and Aripo (1800 hectares). Supporting a rich diversity of fauna, mangroves provide a nurturing environment for invertebrates such as crabs and insects, which are the richest population of any fauna found in all wetlands of Trinidad and Tobago. These invertebrates in turn form the food source for many resident and migrant birds as well as swamp and marine fishes."

Governance as discourse

The current preoccupation with governance is based on the belief that there is always an administrative or managerial 'fix' in the normally difficult affairs of human societies and organisations (Leftwich, 1994). The 1989 World Bank report on Africa argued that governance was 'the exercise of political power to manage a nation's affairs' (Leftwich, 1994). However Leftwich (1994) claims that the Bank's prescription for good governance is naive because it fails to recognise that good governance is a function of state character and capacity, which is in turn a function of politics. The history, practice and theory of the state as an agent is left out of the World Bank definition (Leftwich, 1994).

Paradigmatic shifts in the post-war development discourse produced transformations in the way in which environmental problems were represented. As such within specific historical and institutional arrangements, some conclusions have seemed more tenable than others, and certain interventions have become more legitimate. This is the case in Trinidad where in previous decades the environmental discourse was dismissed as irrelevant to Third World Development. The interviewees considered the discourse on Conservation to be relatively new.

Governmental Five Year plans produced by Planning Departments in many Third World countries were strongly influenced by the development theories of the day and were overtly determined by foreign aid goals. Researchers and policy makers agree that these plan objectives were rarely met. Exposure to shifting development ideologies and their changing vocabulary, sustained sometimes by foreign aid, led to a situation in which some countries were not sure if they even had a strategy for development other than the dutiful recital of development themes that were fashionable at a given point in time. Natural resources existed, primarily to be exploited, either to facilitate trade or for direct appropriation. While there were clear signs of resource degradation, it was relevant to planners only to the extent that it hindered development, and then only marginally so. This is the sentiment echoed by the magistrates dismissing "a few parrots" referred to above. The extent to which Trinidad and Tobago's policies are determined by adherence to the guidelines laid down by external lending agencies is illustrated below:

> "The technocrats continue to destroy agriculture, there is uninformed policy, amazing madness comes out of Ministry of Agriculture. There is no link between what the technocrats know and what is being done. Whatever the

IDB conditionalities are, that is what they do. The IDB does not have field staff, so they accept the report. All these guys get into programs to access money. External lenders - force you to change course, what you do and what you grow is linked to external countries and companies, it is not indigenous. The plans come from failed technocrats. Technocrats who have nothing to do, no plan or strategy, they concoct the figures, and work it until it looks good. People reading the reports know nothing about the industry, they don't think they need to talk to people who know the industry; they rely on technocrats. When it fails, by then the infrastructure is there, they try to correct after the fact. For successful implementation they need to bring in an expert who has no axe to grind. They need to pay them well, let them develop figures, the feasibility study, the planning schedule and the implementation. Who will ask: 'do we need these things'? For the Nariva issue, it is not normal to have so many studies, they didn't get the answer they wanted the first time. The terms of reference. Who they spoke to. Find a way to bypass committees, bring a foreign expert to justify, give different terms of reference, get the result they want. Some of these things could be done yes, but is it more feasible than the alternatives. There is no morality in this society, people want to save their jobs, get a promotion. The Minister promised his friend to buy his agricultural factory; there is a constant racket. There is a lack of respect for ourselves, anything foreigners tell us we believe, especially if it is something we want to hear. "

The extent to which environmental policies were dictated by International bodies is evident from the Interviews below:

Interview 1: "The Tropical Forestry Action Plan[11] gave some direction for protected areas. Nariva was suggested as one of the priority areas. Nothing ever happened but it gave policy directions for the World Bank National Parks proposal. The final decision for the chosen National Parks was 2 parks in the Northern range, Maracas and Matura and Main Ridge in Tobago. 3 parks was the guidelines from the World Bank. The National Park and Watershed project is how it began 6 years ago, the coastal zone component was subsequently left out. The World Bank plan dovetailed with the Tourism Master Plan 1994."

Interview 2: "The National Parks and Wildlife Authority is a component of

---

[11] FAO/Caricom Tropical Forestry Action Programme. 1993. Trinidad and Tobago National Forestry Action Programme (Supplement to the Report of the Country Mission Team - Project Profiles). FAO Investment Centre. March 1993.

the National Watershed Plan, the feasibility study was funded by the World Bank. The World Bank insists on cross-sectoral, multi-disciplinary consultation with stakeholders. It was on that basis that we were able to storm our way into the process. We were also able to use the Wildlife Act, which hadn't yet been drafted to bring our concerns about the National Parks Authority. Some legal minds have removed some of the original spirit of the Acts. "

Interview 3: "The Land Rationalisation study[12] was funded by the IDB. The IDB-funded project was to set up a computerised Land Registration system, and bring the system into the modern era. Since most large projects now have environmental components built in, Sylvia Kacal and Floyd Homer were asked to do a survey in Kernahan. Floyd Homer was from the TT Biological Society and Sylvia Kacal was from CFCA. They asked for 3 potential National Park areas. An objective ranking was done and Maracas, Matura and NE Tobago were chosen. The study found that there was ever decreasing use of resources; fewer people were collecting herbs and vines. Homer and Sylvia Kacal were expected to come up with some little quick projects and suggest some band-aid solutions. All the studies are quick studies; they are never long term, always rush-rush things. The terms of reference for the Homer - Kacal study was only one month; the money was stretched for 3 months since it was considered important. The terms of reference were only for 3 parks. They had hoped for more IDB funding for developing the parks. Now the project is subsumed under the World Bank National Parks and Watershed Project. They were given too little time to do too much work. Molly queried why Nariva was not chosen; it was in the top few but not in the top three. It was based on objective ranking with weightings not emotions. Now there is another project, a quickie, to look at Speyside, Nariva, Caroni, the money comes from GEF."

Kacal and Homer based their report on 28 out of 100 questionnaires looking typical social and cultural characteristics such as ethnicity, religion and income.

---

[12] IDB, 1992. Land Rationalisation and Development Programme. Land Tenure Centre, University of Wisconsin, Madison, Wisconsin, USA, for the Inter-American Development Bank. Non-Reimbursable Technical Co-operation Agreement No. ATN/SF-3159-TT for Trinidad and Tobago. February 1992

Governance: Recommendations and their implementation (?) over the years

All notions of governance focus on relations between state and society at all levels, as well as on governance in non-state actors, such as multinational corporations, non-governmental organisations, trade unions, co-operatives, religious groups, etc (Hardjoeno et al., 1996). Leftwich (1994) considers that the definition of governance currently popular is based on a minimal state, ideal type bureaucracy, respect for human rights, diverse civil society, political pluralism and a distinct separation between economic and political life. Minimalist states tend to downplay social and gender issues, seeks to privatise them and give these back to the community (meaning un-funded housewives) or leave these issues to be attended to by the invisible hand of the market.

Most authorities agree on some of the parameters that constitute good governance:
1. facilitating economic growth by providing an 'enabling environment' encompassing competent public agencies, clear laws which are predictably enforced and reliable information and communication systems;
2. bureaucratic accountability and transparency;
3. ability to resist capture by powerful interest groups;
4. moderate (no?) corruption, and
5. a commitment to reducing poverty, providing basic social services, and ensuring development well-being, which incorporates equality of opportunities, freedom from fear of arbitrary arrest, free speech and free association (Hardjoeno et al., 1996).

Policy decisions are made using concepts, analysis and data; there are people, interest groups and stakeholders involved and the nature of the decision making process can be participatory or top-down (FAO-SEAGA). Policy decisions in Trinidad and Tobago are mainly top-down though that it changing. Policy decisions about agricultural policy are based on technical decisions but are heavily influenced by ethnic politics. National economic policies are never made on the basis of pure economic efficiency because there are always competing power groups and claims on state support (FAO-SEAGA); therefore policies are often designed to meet different social and political goals. The Ministry of Agriculture had its own policy for food self-security, and it was through this policy that the Ministry was obviously captured by the powerful rice lobby through three administrations, PNM, NAR and then PNM again. The term 'capture' is used because the intermediate level institution of TIRGA or the large rice farmers played a mediating role in linking agricultural policy to their direct benefit without any alternatives being considered in public. Interviewers felt that the 'planning' demonstrated by the Ministry was:

" Higgedly piggedly, no one seems to care or develop a plan or develop what seems to be sustainable. The Indian government seems to be supporting Indian farmers or probably the two are in cahoots. Yes maybe they went in under the NAR, but they weren't thrown out when they first started. NAR closed their eyes."

One Minister demonstrated how much influence the large farmers had when he claimed that:

"The rice farmers knew about the O.C.T.A plan. I was in the area frequently and I knew them socially, whenever I went over they had maps and they would lecture me about what the Japanese said. They wanted the land, they expanded, made roads, the small farmers were excluded however and couldn't catch fish in the area."

Policy coherence

Policy makers must respond to a range of support and pressure groups at international, national and sub-national levels with diverse and often contradictory interests. It is partly for this reason that governments often appear to be following 'incoherent', two- or multi-track strategies, degrading the environment with one hand and conserving it with the other. It is also partly for this reason that concepts like 'sustainable development' and 'participation' often remain at the level of rhetoric or 'lip service' and are not translated into concrete policy measures. Additionally laws and policies promoting conservation remain unenforced (Utting, 1994). For example when the National Environment and Conservation Council (NECC) was formed in November 1972, half of its functions related to beach facilities and the other half to the national parks. Primarily NECC was supposed to:

"make recommendations on the development, management and control of national parks," The council was inter-ministerial with a few non-government people (SCAPE included) and chaired by a former Permanent Secretary in the Government's Minister of Planning and Development. Meetings were held and in early 1975 a number of recommendations was made to Government when the council folded up. So far, there appears to be no feedback and no forward motion (Ronald A. Williams, Trinidad Naturalist Vol. 1. No. 6, 1976, pg. 24. Cover Story. What are we doing about National Parks?).

In addition some policies generate certain types of social responses and conflicts, which undermine conservation efforts. An illustration of the type of 'planning' that took place can be found in one internal document of the Ministry of Agriculture, which records that:

> "reconstruction of access roads on private rice-growing lands has been minimal over the years and was usually done in an ad-hoc response to representations made by industrial farmers or their representatives." Ahmad (1991) claims that the development of rice production in the Nariva area was "ad hoc, unplanned and chaotic and the need for some order and regulation is most urgent, as is also the development of a policy for land acquisition and occupation. The farmers have the philosophy that increased production can be achieved by occupying increased areas and not by intensification of production. Therefore, these valuable lands are very poorly utilised and there is much conflict among the farmers for needed resources. The great advantage in developing this area is that most of the land is state owned and the farmers are really squatters. Therefore, in theory, the area can be developed according to an approved physical plan."

In April 1983, the National Physical Development Plan was introduced into Parliament by the Prime Minister and Minister of Finance and Planning, 23 years after the initial planning ordinance, 14 years after the rhetorical recognition of the relevance of spatial issues in the Third Five Year Plan of 1969. The National Physical Development Plan was debated in Parliament and approved on August 15, 1984. The Plan advocated:
1. an overall national growth centre strategy
2. development of a functional hierarchy of urban settlements
3. strong land use controls in agriculture and conservation areas
4. comprehensive rural development in 6 depressed areas including Guayaguayare - Galeota
5. a massive housing and construction program
6. phasing of major development undertakings
7. employment creation (Conway, 1984).

The time gap between the Third Five Year Plan in 1969 and the introduction into Parliament of the National Physical Development Plan tells its own story about the Physical Planning environment. The Plan catered for 'active conservation and other areas to be kept under natural cover which are mainly in the upland areas of the Northern, Central and Southern Ranges, the Caroni Swamp and Tobago's Main Ridge'. The plan on pg. 55 reveals that the 'undeveloped' Nariva Swamp was earmarked to be

'developed': 'the development of a major growth zone in the Mayaro-Galeota area is the most futuristic proposal in the long-term dispersed concentration strategy. The major reasons for the selection of a growth centre in the south-eastern part of the country are:
-its proximity to the undeveloped Nariva Swamp, which can potentially make available 9000 acres for intensive farming and 7,500 acres for livestock rearing. The development of this scheme and the cultivation of other idle lands of good agricultural potential can form the basis of a sizeable food processing and other agro-based industry.
- the existence of other potentials in forestry, fishing and recreation'.

On page 158 the Plan suggests other development activities for the Nariva Swamp:
'The development of the desired resort complexes (of recreational and supporting supply and service activities - including agriculture) should take place in seven principal areas - Tobago, the North Coast of Trinidad, Chaguaramas and the offshore islands, the North - east coast (both south and west of Toco), the Mayaro area, Cedros and the Manzanilla - Nariva Swamp area.
The Nariva Swamp was to be developed in Phase 4 1995 – 2000.

One of the criteria of good governance listed above was not met in the situation of the National Physical Development Plan. This was 'facilitating economic growth by providing an 'enabling environment' encompassing competent public agencies, clear laws which are predictably enforced and reliable information and communication systems'.
Macro-level planning often attempts to advance in one specific field while disregarding negative impacts in others. Environmental strategies are not planned in conjunction with development programmes that would transform specific patterns of accumulation and human settlement that cause environmental damage. The Tropical Forestry Action Plans (TFAP) generally failed to do this with the one exception of Nicaragua (Utting, 1994). The TFAP in Trinidad and Tobago tells its own story:

"In 1991, the senior author was invited to participate in the Tropical Forestry Action Plan (TFAP) and enquired what assessment would be made of the coastal mangrove communities. To his surprise, TFAP had omitted mangroves from the Plan, because foresters had not thought them to be sufficiently important. Once this was rectified a contract was found to inventory swamp forests throughout the Eastern Caribbean, including Trinidad and Tobago. Thus, this lecture could be entitled "The Forgotten Wetlands of Trinidad and Tobago", to underline how little attention has been paid to them and, perhaps more importantly, how little is known about them" (Bacon, 1997).

One reason for the current preoccupation with governance is the belief that there is always an administrative or managerial 'fix' in the normally difficult affairs of human societies and organisations (Leftwich, 1994). Scientists sometimes reveal similar beliefs in scientific, managerial or technological fixes as seen in the quote below:

Quote 1: Examination of a land-use map for the Nariva Swamp will show a multiplicity of competing activities juxtaposed without any apparent logic or design. These competing uses have been regarded as the basis of the management problems facing Nariva and the resolution of existing and potential conflicts has been promoted as a means of ensuring that "Nariva must not die." However, for a radical, rather than superficial solution to the existing conservation impasse, a management strategy is required that recognises the fundamental ecological character of this important natural area (Bacon, 1997). The scientific view is that: "Agriculture in Block B is a good idea if done properly. I would not recommend all of Block B, maybe half and the other half could be a buffer area. It has to be done under conditions of proper land tenure; the haphazard way in which it was done was the problem. They have to agree not to farm in the other areas of the Swamp, those earmarked for other purposes. The NEDECO polder was too large and extended into Bush Bush. Fire has to be kept within the agricultural area and pesticides have to be kept within the agricultural area. Kernahan should not spread up into the rest of the Swamp in a haphazard way."

This managerial fix assumes that putting a managerial structure in place with the relevant university educated managers and technical staff, will result in better control of the behaviour of the squatters who will then peacefully live alongside the snakes and the alligators.

International bodies urge nation states to put their ecological house in order, while at the same time they pressure them to cut government expenditure. Public sector workers are often demoralised and ineffective under these conditions (Utting, 1994). Budget cutting was a reality for some departments as indicated by statements in the 1993 and 1994 Annual Reports of the Forestry Division on their constraints:

'A general lack of adequate transport and regular supply of gas and no aerial surveys dedicated solely to [a conservation] project were undertaken because of lack of funds'.

One interviewee from the Wildlife Section used her personal funds for some of the Community action projects:

"Wildlife had no budget, it was not considered important before NAR came into power. In the NAR days the budget was $40,000 for the whole year, it increased under the NAR. There was literally no money. The Game Wardens pooled money to put gas into the vehicles [they were all men]."

Bacon et al. (1979) gives an indication of lack of government expenditure in the Wildlife Section:

The enforcement of the Conservation of Wildlife Ordinance (1958) for the Bush Bush sanctuary was not very intensive. Regular patrols of the area were not very intensive since there were only three persons (two wardens and a driver) and one jeep to patrol the entire south region of Trinidad. The boundaries were not completely surveyed and marked which made enforcement of legislation difficult. The wardens were not armed whereas the hunters and fishermen were (Bacon et al. 1979: 192).

There is evidence of the lack of financial resources of the Forestry Division and the Wildlife Section. The 1987 Annual Report of the Forestry Division reports that a 15 year Research project on the ecology and biology of the manatee (*Trichechus manatus*), started in December 1983, was by 1987:

downgraded to low priority due to: 1. Non-target status of the species by hunters, 2. Natural protection afforded by habitat, 3. Expensive in terms of man-hours. Allocation to the Forestry Division in 1977 was $8,195,901.00. Expenditure was $9,096,739.91 and Revenue was $985,544.47 (Annual Report of the Forestry Division). In 1992 the Allocation was $718,280.00, Expenditure was $697,051.01 and the 1992 Annual Report contains the statement that 'No monies were allocated under the development vote for 1992'. The Report goes on to list the major constraints of the Division:
1.1. Unavailability of funds to purchase much needed materials and equipment.
1.2. Shortage of vehicles that are mechanically functioning and shortage of funds to purchase fuel.
1.3. Breakdown of telecommunications sets.
1.4. Inadequate and unpredictable release of funds.

1.5. Need for greater equity in the expenditure patterns of the various sections.
1.6. Staffing - Shortage of foresters. Vacant posts for daily rated employees were not filled.

The 1992 Allocation figures for the Forestry Division can be contrasted with the 1984 budget for the Agricultural Engineering and Development Division which implements the Soil and Water Management Programme in rice-producing areas of the Country on behalf of the Extension Division of the Ministry of Agriculture, Lands and Food Production. This is essentially a maintenance programme for rice areas with major thrust on maintenance of watercourses as well as drainage and irrigation systems. The maintenance of access roads and bridges in rice areas also forms an integral part of this programme in an attempt to provide better access to rice growing areas and thereby encourage farmers to grow more rice. The Drainage and Irrigation Section of the Division have developed specific work programmes for Caroni, Penal, Superville, Kernahan and Plum Mitan. The Draft Estimates for the Rice Maintenance programme includes $3,752,238.67 for Personnel Expenditure and $173,560 for Goods and Services. The Wage Expenditure for Plum Mitan 1 in 1984 was more than the Forestry Division's 1992 Allocation.

National wetland policy

The National Policy on Wetland Conservation prepared by the National Wetlands Committee gives an indication of the lack of clarity of Government policy towards wetlands. A quote from this policy is presented below. Quote 1 (taken from Appendix 11 Relevant legal and institutional framework. Background to Policy): There is no written Government policy with regard to wetlands in Trinidad and Tobago. The only clear statements of policy are the facts that Trinidad and Tobago became a Contracting Party to the Ramsar Convention in December 1992, with effect from April 1993 that Nariva Swamp was designated for inclusion in the Ramsar List of Wetlands of International Importance, and the appointment of the National Wetlands Committee in 1995. Otherwise policy and intentions must be inferred from political manifestos, draft legislation, Ministerial speeches, and recent Government actions. The election manifesto of the United National Congress (1995) refers to concerns for natural resources as a crisis. It refers to

"The continued degradation of our physical environment and the wasting of our natural resources continue to increase ---" and implies that this has been a result of a lack of caring in policy implementation, and a tendency to " -- 'cook deals' which are inimical to our society." It states an intention to focus on policies and programmes to target, amongst other factors, "Improvement of the physical and natural environment to support sustainable development for current and future generations."Tourism is important, including "--- the development of inland and marine parks, nature trails, inland and coastal aqua-sports enclaves and resorts -- " for ecotourism. The section on Environment states "Proper management of our natural resources and environment is absolutely essential --" and pledges the UNC to "---develop attitudes which will encourage sustainable utilisation --." It relies on the Environment Management Authority "-- to play a key role in formulating policy, regulation and public awareness on environmental issues." There is however no policy statement on wetlands or any other aspect of Forestry Division's mandate.   Other indications of policy on wetlands are to be found in current draft Forest Resources and National Parks legislation, and the Bucoo Reef Management Plan, which incorporates management of the reef and part of the wetland and sea grass area. However these have not yet become firm reality (National Wetlands Committee, 1996).

Continuing conflicts

Utting (1994) claims that:

> 'In situations where grassroots action has yielded important socio-environmental gains for local groups, this is not the end of the fight. The war is never entirely won. Inegalitarian local structures, co-optation, and ongoing opposition by powerful vested interests means that the pendulum can easily swing back in favour of those who benefit from environmental damage. For this reason it is crucial for local groups not only to remain organised and united, but also to strengthen links with the growing number of outside agents and organisations with an interest in environmental issues.

The idea that the war is not over comes from a report in the Trinidad Guardian Wednesday October 14, 1998, pg. 10:

> " Government has been advised that rice cultivation in Block B of the Nariva Swamp should be immediately stopped and that other agricultural crops should be grown in the wetlands. It has also been told that Block B should be rehabilitated to its original condition and that the man-made water

channels, which even now continue to drain the swamp, should be filled-in without delay. These were the recommendations made to Agriculture Minister, Dr. Reeza Mohammed, by 18 separate committees mandated to review the Environmental Assessment (EIA) done by the Institute of Marine Affairs. The last line is a telling one: 18 separate committees were asked to look at the EIA...18 separate committees.... 18.

The Council of Presidents for the Environment (COPE) held a panel discussion on the Nariva Swamp on the evening of Oct 14, 1998 at the University of the West Indies. The Panelists were Molly Gaskin, Theresa Akaloo, Peter Bacon, Motilal Lal, Guptee Lutchmedial and Dave McIntosh. Kamau Akili from Environment Tobago was the moderator. Theresa Akaloo objected to the "biased" panel and Bally Seepersad (consultant to the rice farmers) was allowed to join the panel. The event was reported on by Lisa Allen-Agostini in the Sunday Express of October 18, 1998 (pg 3). The article had the headline "Gaskin knocks $7m subsidy for 'dog rice'." "They are not feeding the nation…the rice is not table rice." Gaskin also claimed that the farmers received $7 million in subsidies annually and got soft loans from the ADB which they never repaid. Theresa Akaloo rebutted and apparently so did members of the audience. All present asked for the EIA to be made public by Dr. Reeza Mohammed (Paul, 1998). Theresa may have been using the maternal care rhetoric in her claim to be "feeding the nation" and MacGregor (2004) claims that the ecofeminist care ethic has many dangers including that the need to protect and care for a particular other (say a child) can lead to actions that are harmful to generalized others. This can have an impact on ecological politics (i.e. NIMBY).

In February 1998 some of the large farmers were growing rice on lands leased to them by Caroni but Theresa Akaloo said that 500 acres given to them was not enough… [she said that] the survival of Nariva is not uncompatible with the growing of rice in the wetlands and that the farmers were not against preserving the swamp (Rostant, 1998).

The EIA forced an economic discussion of environmental impacts, an analysis of growth/development vs. environmental issues and to quantify the subsidy to the large-scale rice farmers which amounted to TT$4,249,763. The rice planting activity contributed only marginally to the macro-economy, amounting to about .07% of country GDP or about 2.37% of agriculture's contribution to GDP. The rice farming activities only marginally improved employment opportunities in the local Nariva communities (IMA, 1998).

However it seems that the female activists and volunteers have not allowed themselves to be intimidated by Ministers with patriarchal attitudes:

> Interview 2: " I heard there was a lot of bacchanal in the meetings when the Minister asked for recommendations on the swamp and the EIA. Certain members of the WLCC were not invited but heard about it and turned up anyway and were asked to leave."

Conclusion

This study documented and evaluated state policy toward agricultural resource use and settlement in the Nariva area (e.g. agricultural policy, settlement policy, infrastructural development, tourism policy, political context, allocation of land rights). Governance comprises of State, local and community levels, however the analysis focused on the macro level since this is where the power to make things happen lies. Decisions are made at this level for the entire nation, and international events and forces are mediated at the macro level for the nation (FAO-SEAGA).

The following can be concluded:

• There are environmental ideologies and discourses that affect the Nariva swamp. There is a perceived crisis in leadership and governance in Trinidad and Tobago on environmental issues that environmental organisations are seeking to fill through links to international organisations and funding agencies. The granting of international recognition to Nariva as a Ramsar site affected the ecological status of the swamp, the political status of the swamp, and the livelihood of the communities, the type of research being conducted and the beneficiaries of research funding

• There has there been a historical predisposition to favour commercial use of the swamp rather than ecologically sustainable use. There are indications that this predisposition is a gendered one.

Appendix 1: supporting documents

1990s situation

DRAFT. REPUBLIC OF TRINIDAD AND TOBAGO FOOD AND AGRICULTURE POLICY 1994 - 1996 WHITE PAPER. MINISTRY OF AGRICULTURE, LANDS AND MARINE RESOURCES. MARCH 1994.

Pg. 3. SECTOR RESOURCES
A. NATURAL RESOURCES
AGRICULTURAL LANDS
WETLANDS
WATER RESOURCES
FOREST RESOURCES
FISHERIES RESOURCES

WETLANDS

The major wetlands of ecological importance are located in Trinidad and include such areas as the Nariva Swamp (6,234 hectares); Caroni Swamp (5,611 hectares); South Oropouche Lagoon (5,642 hectares) and Fishing Pond (1,220 hectares). Mangrove forests make up a substantial proportion of most wetlands, except for manmade lakes and the inland savannahs, which include, Erin (40 hectares) and Aripo (1800 hectares). Supporting a rich diversity of fauna, mangroves provide a nurturing environment for invertebrates such as crabs and insects, which are the richest population of any fauna found in all wetlands of Trinidad and Tobago. These invertebrates in turn form the food source for many resident and migrant birds as well as swamp and marine fishes.

Biodiversity Studies

Alistair Duguid and his University of Glasgow colleagues conducted an environmental impact study on the Nariva rice paddies to judge their impact on fish communities. They did a preliminary survey of the fish species in the pristine Swamp versus the surrounding paddy fields over a few weeks in the rainy season, in daylight. Their netting technique only worked well in the paddy channels.

Table 5. Physical data from the four sites (Duguid et al., 1996)

Site	Substrate type	Mean depth (m)
Pristine swamp	Undecomposed leaves and sticks. Black mud	0.8
Bush-bush channel	Black mud	1.0
Controlled paddies	Brown mud	0.3
Unofficial paddies	Brown mud	0.7

Table 6. Catch data from the four sites (Duguid et al., 1996)

Site	No. of individuals	No. of species	Fish density (individuals/m3)	Biomass density (g/ m3)
Pristine swamp	65	3	2.26	3.47
Bush-bush channel	28	5	0.97	0.61
Controlled paddies	30	7	1.67	19.75
Unofficial paddies	155	3	6.15	9.75

There was more food for fish in the paddies because the oxygenated mud supported more invertebrates. The pink finned sardine (*Astyanax bimaculatus*) composed 97% of the catch in the unofficial paddy channel.

Nariva swamp reclamation schemes

The information in this section is modified from IMA 1991, FAO 1985, the original documents, and other sources.

NO NAME 2 (Agristudio ??)

1. INTRODUCTION

This Plum Mitan Rice Scheme Rehabilitation Feasibility Study describes the climatological and the hydrological investigations and methods used to calculate design discharges and main hydrological features. The Project Area is located in the centre of the eastern part of the island and lying at 10 degrees 27 ' N latitude and 61 degrees 07 ' W longitude. The Project Area covers about 420 hectares and is situated in a flat, low lying plain of Nariva Swamp, between the Perimeter Cut in the east, the Petit Pool Cut in the north, Cuche and Canque Cut in the west, and the Jagroma Cut in the south.

pg. i. Summary and Conclusions

Trinidad and Tobago, though an agricultural country - suffers from the scarcity of suitable agricultural land for the development of the farm sector. The Nariva Swamp is the only virgin area of any size, which remains undeveloped and attracts the attention of the Government and its planning agencies. The project presented here is originally the conception and proposals put forward for the development of the Nariva Swamp by the Overseas Development Agency of the Government of Japan. The Team examined the O.C.T.A's project and put forward a revised version of that project. The general aspects of the design and construction of the engineering works were sound and practicable, and no significant changes were made to that area of the original O.C.T.A project. An increase of 15% has been computed into costs and prices to bring these up to 1972 levels. The preliminary appraisal did not think the choice of dry season crops was satisfactory, the projected rice yields were too low, and the livestock project was discarded as uneconomical. The rate of return to the O.C.T.A project was not more than 8% and on that basis the project could be considered less than feasible. Subsequently, using more up-to-date yield data for rice, and replacing the soya bean/maize rotation with dry season rice and pulses, the Team arrived at a more realistic cropping programme and one, which is more practicable. Even so, this new cropping plan is conservative - but allows flexibility. Dry season crops could be readily varied in the first few years if, for instance, irrigation efficiency is less than planned, to shift from rice to pulses wherever necessary. In addition, if market conditions warrant, certain other cash crops such as watermelons, sweet potatoes, sweet peppers and other vegetables, which give high returns per hectares, could be carefully introduced. At full development, the project should produce an equivalent to 63% of current imports of rice and 25% of current imports of peas and beans - a total of $7.5 million. From year 9, the project would settle 730 farm families with 5.26 hectares of developed and irrigated land. The average farm family size in Trinidad is estimated at seven persons of whom four would contribute labour on the farm. The net annual labour and management income per farmers at full development compares favourably with average urban/industrial incomes of TT$4600.

The economic rate of return of the project is estimated at 12%. The net income per farm at full development would be over $6600 TT per year ($4,600 per year is the average net urban income). At full development the project would supply approximately 63% of current volume of rice imports and 25% of the current volume of imports of peas and beans. The project will settle 730 families with an average size of seven members and create over 1,000 full-time job opportunities.

Table 7. Farm net returns Agristudio report

TT $	YEAR 6	YEAR 11	YEAR 14
5 hectares wet season paddy	2550	4015	4015
2.5 hectares dry season paddy	2355	1723	1723
2.5 hectares dry season pulses	-	275	905
TOTAL	4905	6013	6643

Total established cost of the project would approximate TT$ 29.5 million, of which TT $15.8 million could be contributed from local public resources and the balance of TT $13.7 million could be sought as a soft loan from an International Lending Agency. Operating and Management Costs after completion of Stage 1 (1150 hectares) would be about TT$44,000 annually, increasing to TT$121,000 after full development in year 11 (3650 hectares).

Table 8. The Nariva Swamp Development Authority from the Agristudio report

Ministry of Agriculture	Extension Division - Nariva / Mayaro
Ministry of Works	Drainage & Reclamation Division - Nariva/ Mayaro
Agricultural Development Bank	Eastern Branch Office
Dept. of Cooperative Development	Cooperative Development Office - Nariva/Mayaro
Nariva Agricultural Cooperative	Executive Committee

The Nariva Agricultural Cooperative would include all the farmers of the project - though not limited to the project - and would be responsible for the advance of credit obtained from the Agricultural Development Bank and with general cooperative enterprise including the machinery pool, the supply of farm inputs, and the marketing of farm produce.

Build up of Settlement and Farming Area. Cultivated Area:

Each farm would be allotted 5.00 hectares in the developed area of which 2.50 hectares would be irrigated in the dry season after full development.

Research, Seed and Nursery Area:

An area of 0.27 hectares per farm would be organized in a favoured location into a 200 hectares area for research and for the production of seed and rice seedlings at cost plus an amount computed into the charge equivalent to the rent of 0.27 hectares

House and Home Garden:

Each farm family would be allotted 0.41 hectares (1.00 ac.) in the village settlement. The settlement site would be selected in the higher land bordering the Swamp project area. This area allows each farm family about 0.30 to 0.35 hectares (3/4 to 7/8 ac.) for home garden cultivation.

III. THE PROJECT AREA

4,450 hectares (11,000 ac.) selected for the project.

pg. 4. LAND UTILISATION   GENERAL

Most of the Nariva area remains an unused wasteland.

The Plum Mitan Rice Expansion Scheme is a drainage and irrigation project covering 490 hectares (1200 ac.) in the Northwestern section of the Swamp. This was established in 1960. Briefly it was designed to intercept the excess water from the watershed by three channels - the Jagroma cut, the Cuche cut and the Petit Poole cut - in the rainy season using the same channels to irrigate by directed stream flow in the dry season. The lack of really effective stream flow in the dry season and the lack of a storage reservoir coupled with a complete absence of continued organization and management allows only a minimum use of the scheme area - about 120 hectares (300 acres) of paddy being planted in the rainy season. Our group recommends that the rehabilitation of the Plum Mitan Scheme should be given priority either within the Nariva Project or without that project. The rehabilitation of the Plum Mitan Scheme is included in the project as a pilot sub-project in which the necessary trials are made in order to define and delimit the best development pattern for the area as a whole.

IV. THE PROJECT

The project is basically to control water. The drainage scheme covers the project area, and the watershed area adjacent to the project area, totalling approximately 4,450 hectares (11,000 acres) which are the areas at elevations lower than 33.5 m (110 feet TGR). The tables are based on 5 hectares of paddy.

Table 9. Agristudio report cropping plan

Year	Hectares	Wet season paddy	Dry season paddy	Dry season pulses
1 - 5	-	-	-	-
6 - 9	1150	1150	1150	-
10	2650	2650	2650	-
11 AND AFTER	3650	3650	1825	1825

Table 10. Agristudio report crop yields and returns

Year	Wet season	Wet season	Dry season	Dry season	Dry season	Dry season
	Paddy	Paddy	Paddy	Paddy	Pulses	Pulses
	Kg. Per hectares	Metric tons/project	Kg. Per hectares	Metric tons/project	Kg. Per hectares	Metric tons/project
1 - 5	-	-	-	-	-	-
6	5000	5750	4000	4600		-
7	5500	6325	4500	5175		-
8	6000	6900	5000	5750		-
9	6500	7475	5000	5750		-
10	6500	17225	5000	13250		-
11	6500	23725	5000	9125	1130	2062
12	6500	23725	5000	9125	1320	2409
13	6500	23725	5000	9125	1480	2701
14 - 25	6500	23725	5000	9125	1690	3084

Table 11. Agristudio report projected returns

Year	Wet season paddy	Dry season paddy	Dry season pulses	Total(000 $TT)
1 - 5	-	-	-	
6	1121	897	-	2018
7	1233	1009	-	2242
8	1346	1121	-	2467
9	1458	1121	-	2579
10	3359	2548	-	5943
11	4626	1779	928	7333
12	4626	1779	1084	7489
13	4626	1779	1215	7620
14 - 25	4626	1779	1308	7793

Table 12. Agristudio report net returns

Year	Wet season paddy	Wet season paddy	Dry season paddy	Dry season paddy	Dry season pulses	Dry season pulses	Annual project total
(000 $TT)	Per hectares $	Project	Per hectares $	Project	Per hectares $	Project	Total
1 - 5	-	-	-	-	-	-	-
6	510	587	471	542	-	-	1129
7	608	699	580	667	-	-	1366
8	705	811	689	792	-	-	1603
9	803	923	689	792	-	-	1715
10	803	2128	689	1826	-	-	3954
11	803	2931	689	1257	110	201	4389
12	803	2931	689	1257	196	358	4546
13	803	2931	689	1257	268	490	4188
14 - 25	803	2931	689	1257	362	661	4849

Table 13. Agristudio report farm net income

Year	No. Farms	Wet season paddy (5 ac. Paddy)	Dry season paddy	Dry season pulses	Total TT$
6	230	$2550	(5 hectares) 2355	-	4905
7	230	3040	2900	-	5940
8	230	3525	3445	-	6970
9	230	4015	3445	-	7460
10	468	4015	3445	-	7460
11	730	4015	(2.5 hectares) 1723	275	6013
12	730	4015	1723	490	6228
13	730	4015	1723	670	6408
14 - 25	730	4015	1723	905	6643

F. Project Costs

The total project costs amount to TT $30 million, which excludes the interest during construction of TT $2.9 million. Project construction is to be executed in two stages. During the first stage, which will be completed in five (5) years time the Cocal Reservoir interceptor drain, part of the irrigation canal to serve 1,150 hectares, a waterway (Cocal Cut), part of the irrigation canal to serve 1,150 hectares, a waterway (Cocal Cut), part of the drainage systems - access roads, spillway and outlet works would be constructed. This would require and outlay of some TT $5.9 million. The second stage would take another five years and would entail the construction of the irrigation and drainage systems, the Nariva Regulating Reservoir, Barrage and Estuary Works and Serviceways. This would cost TT $10.5 million. The total project construction costs will be TT $16.4 million, forty-seven percent of which would be borrowed funds. Associated costs, which are part of the project costs, are listed in the table below.

Table 14. Agristudio report associated costs

Particulars($ TT)	First stage	Second stage	Total
Land Improvement	740	1610	2350
Settlement houses, etc.	800	1960	2760
Training and Extension	250	-	250
Cooperative facilities	667	1196	1863
Machinery (field cultivation)	736	1461	2197
Others; Annual costs, Consulting services	108	196	
Operation and maintenance	44	121	
Replacement of gates on 25th year	460	380	
Interest during construction, 6%	-	-	2900

Trinidad Naturalist coverage of the Nariva Swamp

Trinidad Naturalist VOL 1. NO. 6. 1976

Cover photo: Bush Bush Wildlife Sanctuary. Inside photo pg 25. Caption: part of sanctuary destroyed by woodcutters.

pg. 24. Cover story: what are we doing about national parks? By Ronald A. Williams

...When the National Environment and Conservation Council (NECC) was formed in November 1972, half of its functions related to beach facilities and the other half to the national parks. Primarily NECC was supposed to "make recommendations on the development, management and control of national parks," The council was inter-ministerial with a few non-government people (SCAPE included) and chaired by a former Permanent Secretary in the Government's Minister of Planning and Development. Meetings were held and in early 1975 a number of recommendations was made to Government when the council folded up. So far, there appears to be no feedback and no forward motion.

Trinidad Naturalist VOL 1. NO. 9 PG. 9. SURVIVAL

Trinidad Naturalist VOL 2. NO. 6 NARIVA THE WILDEST PLACE OF ALL, COVER PICTURE AND INSIDE STORY

Trinidad Naturalist VOL. 3. NO. 4. PG. 41. STORY ON FORESTERS

Trinidad Naturalist VOL. 4. NO. 4. PG. 10. INTERVIEW WITH KAMAL MOHAMMED

Trinidad Naturalist VOL. 5. NO. 7. PG 22. IN SEARCH OF THE MANATEE

Trinidad Naturalist VOL. 7. NO. 2. PG. 20. CATTLE IN BUSH BUSH

Trinidad Naturalist VOL. 7. NO. 3. PG. 16. NARIVA NATIONAL PARK

Trinidad Naturalist VOL. 6. NO. 5. SPECIAL ISSUE ON CARONI SWAMP

Overview of Forestry Division activities in Nariva Swamp

BACON ET AL., 1979

pg. 192

The enforcement of the Conservation of Wildlife Ordinance (1958) for the Bush Bush sanctuary was not very intensive. Regular patrols of the area were not very intensive since there were only three persons (two wardens and a driver) and one jeep to patrol the entire south region of Trinidad. The boundaries were not completely surveyed and marked which made enforcement of legislation difficult. The wardens were not armed whereas the hunters and fishermen were.

FORESTRY REPORT 1

ANNUAL REPORT OF THE FORESTRY DIVISION FOR THE YEAR 1987

Table 15. List of legally constituted and demarcated forest reserves

Name	Hectares at 1/1/96	Date of Proclamation	Hectares at 31/12/1987
Brigand Hill	127.9	8-12-25	127.9
Manzanilla Windbelt	1782.2	16-2-22	1782.2
Manzanilla Extension	383.2	11-2-55	383.2
Nariva Windbelt	2528.9	12-3-54	2528.9

Sixty one (61) State Game Licenses (S.G.L.) were sold at the Biche District Revenue Office in 1987. Revenue collected was $305.00. At Mayaro, 247 Licenses were sold and revenue collected was $735.00. Twenty Forest Offences were recorded at Mayaro, fines collected amounted to $1505.90. Twelve forest offences were recorded at Biche and $666.64 in fines were paid.

FORESTRY REPORT 2

PLAN FOR A SYSTEM OF NATIONAL PARKS AND OTHER PROTECTED AREAS IN TRINIDAD AND TOBAGO. K.D. Thelen and S. Faizool**Error! Bookmark not defined.**

FORESTRY DIVISION, MINISTRY OF AGRICULTURE LANDS AND FISHERIES, PORT OF SPAIN, TRINIDAD. MAY 1980. TECHNICAL DOCUMENT FORESTRY DIVISION/ORGANISATION OF AMERICAN STATES PROJECT ON THE ESTABLISHMENT OF A SYSTEM OF NATIONAL PARKS AND OTHER PROTECTED AREAS

Table 16. Thelen and Faizool recommendation for Bush Bush national park

NAME	SIZE OF AREA (ha.)	DATE OF ESTABLISHMENT	OUTSTANDING FEATURES	PRESENT CONDITION	RECOMMENDATIONS
Bush Bush	1554	1968	Large fresh water swamp with a wide variety of species	Substantial human interference in the form of hunting and poaching. Instances of squatting timber extraction, and fishing for cascadura Some fire damage during the dry season; however, damages not considered significant	Area to be expanded to include mangrove swamp and coastal areas and be managed as a National Park.

ANNUAL REPORT OF THE FORESTRY DIVISION, 1977

SUMMARY OF GAME OFFENCES FOR THE YEAR 1977/78

27 cases reported, 16 fined, 6 reprimanded and discharged, 5 dismissed. Conviction Royalty $1,670.00.

Table 17. Forestry Division allocation expenditure and revenue 1977

A.	ALLOCATION	
	RECURRENT	2,990,311.00
	DEVELOPMENT PROGRAMME	5,088,590.00
	EXTRAORDINARY	117,000.00
	TOTAL	8,195,901.00
B.	EXPENDITURE	
	PERSONAL EMOLUMENTS & TRAVELLING	1,857,935.93
	RECURRENT	2,884,443.38
	DEVELOPMENT PROGRAMME	4,314,115.98
	EXTRAORDINARY	40,244.62
	TOTAL	9,096,739.91
C.	REVENUE	
	SALE OF FOREST PRODUCE	695,564.80
	SALE OF PRODUCE FROM BRICKFIELD FOREST INDUSTRIES (BFI)	274,973.50
	SALE OF GAME PERMITS, SAWMILL LICENCES & FINES RE: OFFENCES	15,006.17
	TOTAL	985,544.47

ANNUAL REPORT OF THE FORESTRY DIVISION 1987

RESEARCH TITLE: ECOLOGY AND BIOLOGY OF THE MANATEE (*Trichechus manatus*)

DURATION   LONG TERM 15 YEARS

INCEPTION   DECEMBER 1983

OBJECTIVES

1. Obtain basic information on the ecology of the manatee in Trinidad

2. Preparation of management plans to ensure the survival of this endangered species.

ACHIEVEMENTS   REMARKS

i. Project downgraded to low priority due to:

1. Non-target status of the species by hunters.

2. Natural protection afforded by habitat.

3. Expensive in terms of man-hours.

....

FORESTRY DIVISION ANNUAL REPORT 1988. pg. 33.

Plum Mitan, Nariva has waterbirds and howler monkeys and suggested recreation activities for the area are birdviewing, photography and artwork.

FORESTRY DIVISION ANNUAL REPORT 1992.   Administrative Section

Fines collected from wildlife offences, 51 persons were convicted: total fines $24,375.

Instruments were laid on December 21, 1992 with respect to the declaration of the Nariva Swamp as a RAMSAR site.

FINANCES RECURRENT EXPENDITURE   ALLOCATION $718,280.00

EXPENDITURE $697,051.01

No monies were allocated under the development vote for 1992.

Major constraints of the Division

1.1. Unavailability of funds to purchase much needed materials and equipment.

1.2. Shortage of vehicles that are mechanically functioning and shortage of funds to purchase fuel.

1.3. Breakdown of telecommunications sets.

1.4. Inadequate and unpredictable release of funds.

1.5. Need for greater equity in the expenditure patterns of the various sections.

1.6. Staffing - Shortage of foresters. Vacant posts for daily rated employees were not filled.

ANNUAL REPORT OF THE FORESTRY DIVISION, 1993

Fifteen permits were given to enter Bush Bush Wildlife Sanctuary.

pg. 65.

The Trinidad and Tobago Field Naturalists Club undertook a research project on the status of the manatee in Nariva Swamp with the assistance of the Wildlife Section.

The San Juan Rotary Club collaborated on the conservation of the manatee in Nariva Swamp, Manazanilla.

Thomas Peake and Co. Ltd., donated $2,000.00 for gasoline and oil towards patrols for the Nariva Swamp.

pg. 66

CONVENTION ON WETLANDS OF INTERNATIONAL IMPORTANCE ESPECIALLY AS WATERFOWL HABITAT (RAMSAR, 1971)

Trinidad and Tobago acceded to the RAMSAR Convention in April 1993, with Nariva Swamp being designated as the country's RAMSAR site. An application was made to its Wetland Conservation Fund for assistance with Nariva Swamp but the proposal did not meet with success. Application for the Monitoring Procedure to be applied for Nariva Swamp was made, and this will provide technical assistance for conservation of this wetland.

pg. 68.   DETAILS OF RESEARCH

1. DEVELOPMENT AND MANAGEMENT OF WILDLIFE SANCTUARIES

DURATION: LONG TERM   INCEPTION: 1991

OBJECTIVES:

1.1. To undertake research to address wildlife management needs and objectives.

1.2. To manage natural habitat at Bush Bush, Trinity Hills, Central Range, Hollis Reservoir and Caroni Swamp to support optimal wildlife population levels for ecological, recreational and aesthetic values.

1.3. To manipulate habitat to create ideal conditions for increased wildlife population levels.

1.4. To protect and manage critical habitats necessary to sustain endemic, endangered, threatened and migratory wildlife species.

ACCOMPLISHMENTS

i. The entire Nariva Swamp was declared a prohibited area under Section 2 of the Forests Act, Chapter 66:01 in May 1993.

ii. Boundaries within Nariva Swamp were identified - the Sanctuary and Proposed National Park.

111. Habitat evaluations in the squatted areas of Bush Bush Wildlife Sanctuary were done.

iv. Two comprehensive reports were written on the extent of squatting and its consequences to the environment of Nariva Swamp, and submitted to the Ministry of Agriculture, Land and Marine Resources.

CONSTRAINTS/REMARKS:

1. Inadequate vehicular transport hampered progress.

2. Widespread illegal activity continues in the Bush Bush Wildlife Sanctuary, and as such, work was severely curtailed.

MANGEMENT OF COASTAL AND MARINE WILDLIFE RESOURCES OF INTERNATIONAL AND NATIONAL SIGNIFICANCE

DURATION: 3 - 5 years INCEPTION: 1991

OBJECTIVES: 3.3 Protect and manage the areas

ACCOMPLISHMENTS

1. Trinidad and Tobago's accession to the RAMSAR Convention took place in May 1993, with the Nariva Swamp designated as this country's RAMSAR site.

2. A formal application was made for RAMSAR's Monitoring Procedure to be applied for Nariva Swamp (this would provide technical assistance in determining management strategies for the Swamp).

CONSTRAINTS/REMARKS

1. A general lack of adequate transport and regular supply of gas.

2. No aerial surveys dedicated solely to this project were undertaken because of lack of funds.

pg. 40. Highlights of the year

1. A visit from a technical officer of the RAMSAR Bureau, and the inception of the Monitoring Procedure for Nariva Swamp.

2. The continuing eviction of squatters in Nariva Swamp.

7. Blossoming of the project on the conservation of the West Indian manatee, and stimulated public interest for their successful involvement in this effort.

283 permits were issues to enter Bush Bush Wildlife Sanctuary / Nariva Swamp Protected Area.

Thomas Peake and Co. Ltd.,. donated $4000.00 for gasoline and oil towards patrols for Nariva Swamp.

pg. 48.

Convention on Wetlands of International Importance especially as waterfowl habitat (RAMSAR, 1971).

In 1994, close collaboration was undertaken with the RAMSAR Bureau with the visit of their technical officer for the Neotropical Region in October, Dr. Montserrat Carbonnel, a specific objective of the visit being to hold preliminary discussions regarding the implementation of the Monitoring Procedure at the Nariva Swamp RAMSAR site. This was deemed by the Scientific and Technical Review Panel of the Bureau to be one of their five (5) priority projects for 1994, and field assessments are scheduled for March 1995. Visits were also made by Dr. Carbonnel to other wetlands in Trinidad, and she recommended that applications for inclusion of some of these on the RAMSAR list be made. It was suggested that application be made to RAMSAR'S Wetland Conservation Fund to facilitate the necessary collection of data on these sites, and it is expected that this will be done in 1995.

IUCN has made offers of assistance for Nariva Swamp.

RESEARCH POLICY STRATEGIES

Management of Coastal and Marine Wildlife.

Resources of International and National Significance

DURATION: 3 - 5 years INCEPTION: 1991

OBJECTIVE

3.[out of 3 in total]. To protect and manage the areas and their wildlife resources, particularly those that are proposed as RAMSAR sites under the Convention on Wetlands of International Importance.

STATUS OF THE MANATEE (*Trichechus manatus*)

DURATION: 15 years   INCEPTION: 1983   pg. 57.

Review of the objective and proposals comprising this programme was undertaken in 1994, and a Project Proposal for the Research, Conservation and Management of *Trichechus manatu*s in Trinidad was compiled for the revised programme.

OBJECTIVES:

-To determine the habitat requirements of the manatee. This involves the compilation of floral and faunal visits as well as analysis of important abiotic parameters.

-To determine the status and distribution of this species in Trinidad.

-To conduct research into the biology of the manatee, including the feeding habitats.

-To conduct a comprehensive literature review and compile in a library system.

-To assess the ecotourism potential of this species.

-To conduct effective educational and public awareness programmes, both at national and community levels.

ACCOMPLISHMENTS:

1. Habitat assessment

a. A complete floral list has been compiled for Big Pond, Manzanilla.

b. Hydrological analysis of Big Pond, Nariva River, and the North Oropouche River was conducted.

c. Incomplete faunal records for Big Pond were compiled.

2. POPULATION STATUS AND DISTRIBUTION

a. Over forty (40) field trips were conducted to Big Pond, Manzanilla, where data indicates a minimum population of five (5), including at least one (1) sub-adult.

b. Three (3) field trips were conducted to the North Oropouche River where the population is estimated to be at least two (2).

c. One (1) field trip was conducted to the Nariva River, but a reliable population estimate cannot yet be made. It should be noted that this population and the population in Big Pond should possibly be considered as one population, as it has been hypothesised (but not conclusively proven) that a connection exists between these two water bodies, and is traversed by the manatee seeking refuge in the larger Nariva River during the dry season.

d. Two (2) field trips were made to the Ortoire River with an estimated minimum population of two (2) recorded.

Comment on RAMSAR, 1996.

Final Report, Monitoring Procedure, Nariva Swamp, Trinidad and Tobago. RAMSAR convention. Gland, Switzerland.

The RAMSAR Convention's prologue states: Recognizing the interdependence of Man and his environment; considering the fundamental ecological functions of wetlands as regulators of water regimes and as habitats supporting a characteristic flora and fauna, especially waterfowl; being convinced that wetlands constitute a resource of great economic, cultural, scientific and recreational value the loss of which would be irreparable; recognizing that waterfowl in their seasonal migrations can transcend frontiers and so should be regarded as an international resource. RAMSAR claims that combining far-sighted policies with co-ordinated action can ensure the conservation of wetlands and their flora and fauna. The Final report of the RAMSAR Convention Monitoring Procedure for the Nariva Swamp, RAMSAR, 1996 can be considered one of the most comprehensive studies. This report resulted from listing of Nariva on the Montreux record, which is a register of sites where changes in ecological character have occurred, are occurring or are likely to occur as a result of technological developments, pollution or other human interference. The Monitoring procedure aims to bring about the steps necessary for the removal of the site from the Montreux Record. As a result of the illegal activities in the Swamp the GORTT asked the RAMSAR Bureau to apply the Monitoring procedure and organize a mission to the Swamp to analyze the extent of the environmental problems and make a set of recommendations for action. This document and its recommendations are likely to be used by both the GORTT and environmentalists as the basis for all future work in the Nariva Swamp.

The Report emphasized that rice farming costs were too high and that many farmers have complete crop failures due to weeds, shortage of water and/or lack of machinery. The report recommended the preparation of a management plan, an economic evaluation and an EIA of Sector B, in additional to hydrological and hydraulic studies to guide conservation and wise use. The report emphasized including the communities in all studies and in all future decision making and planning. The report also recommended a socio-economic study of the communities surrounding Nariva to identify the community's requirements for support in capacity building and institutional strengthening, and developing the wise use of forest and swamp products, etc., nationwide. The report also highlighted agricultural problems for instance, farmers are paid based on the quality of their rice, however the available Columbian varieties cannot reach Grade A, or 0% chalkiness, and produce unfilled grains (blanks)

(RAMSAR, 1996). Sylvia Kacal made the comment that she and other environmentalists had to temper some of the Reports recommendations before final publication. The report does seem to emphasize waterfowl and wading birds in its recommendations for buffalo grazing. Is buffalo grazing compatible with the other flora and fauna, for instance the manatee? What is the carrying capacity of the Swamp for buffalo? What is the economic size of a buffalo-cheese making operation? Cheese making depends on electricity, water and other infrastructure that is missing from the Nariva site in the early 1990s an Italian-operated cheese factory was driven in to bankruptcy due to New Zealand cheese dumping.

The Report recommends a dairy for the Sand Hill site that is reported by environmentalists to be an iguana breeding ground and gives a panoramic view of the Swamp. Electric fencing was recommended for an area with no household electricity. A comprehensive proposal was made for water management that does not seem to fit our culture. Would an objective, impartial manager be found for this plan? The RAMSAR report recommended paying US$40,000 to access CIAT rice technology there are surely cheaper options. There was also a questionable statement that Guyana could not meet the rice needs of Trinidad, based on the professional opinion of one [disinterested ?] source.

Economic aspects, draft technical report for the nariva management plan/EIA

Activity 2. Estimation of the non-user value of the nariva swamp   (Dr. C. Pemberton)

User values from the utilization of the natural products from the Swamp, as well as recreation.

-non-user values - existence value that individuals may receive from just knowing that the Swamp is there; and

-bequest values from knowing that the Swamp will be there (or exist) in the future. So that future generations will receive its benefits.

Non-user value for Nariva Swamp

$290.76 mean annual non-user value

The mean aggregative value over all households $79,042,212.

Social non-user value $TT 608 million.

User value of Nariva

1. Short term user value

a. Economic activity in Block B prior to large-scale rice farming

-conch, cucumber, watermelon, cascadura.

Total revenue from Block B before large-scale rice farming $TT 846,647.

Total costs of inputs $TT 279,037.

Total employment from above : 65 persons

Economic activities in Block A and Kernahan

Watermelon $11 million, $6 million net revenue

Rice $1.8 million   Bodie $2.3 million

Total value crop production $15.7 million

Total net revenue $8.2 million

Assumed 68 full-time fishermen catching conch- $163,800 and cascadura-$377,520. Total sales $ 541,320. Total net $353,820.

Overall agricultural activity crop production and fishing = $16.2 million ($16,233,133) - total value of production

Total net revenue $8.6 million ($8,578,473)   Total family members = 546

Hired for farming in Block A and Kernahan = 52

Large Scale Rice Growing in Block B

Large scale rice farmers - 2 crops of rice on 950 hectares in Block B.

Annual value of rice production estimated at $TT 11,172,000

Total net revenue to farmers of $TT 2,392,100

Cash cost of inputs being $TT 8,779,900

Total cash cost of large-scale rice production was $TT 1.54/kg based on yield of 3000 kg/hectares. 194 persons hired per year by large-scale rice farmers
pg. 27.

The large rice farmers received an implied land subsidy of $TT $16,107.00 (950 /1.22 * $21.46) because they did not pay rent for the land they used in Block B. In addition, an implied subsidy for water of $TT 914.48 / hectares or $TT 868,756.00 for the 950 hectares, farmed were obtained by farmers. The price support payment (subsidy) for rice paddy was $1.01 /kg of paddy. The price subsidy per crop of rice in Block B therefore would be $TT 2,878,500 (3000 * $1.01 * 950) for the 2 crops per year, the total price subsidy was $5,757,000. The overall subsidy for land rent, water and price of paddy was calculated at $TT 6,641,863 ($TT 16,107 + $TT 868,756 + $TT 5,757,000).

Table 18. Net Revenue per crop from large scale rice farming in Block B

ITEM	VALUE
Acreage in hectares	950
Cash cost per hectares	$4621
Total cash cost	$4,389,950
Revenue per hectares	$5880
Total Revenue	$5,586,000
Net Revenue	$1,196,050

pg. 28.

The Business Community during Large-scale Rice Farming in Block B

In the Reconnaissance Survey, it was reported that no new businesses were established as a result of large-scale rice farming in Block B, nor did the existing businesses reap any great benefit as a result of the activities taking place. The large-scale rice farmers brought machinery, equipment, chemicals, fertilizers, and other supplies from outside the Biche / Plum Mitan district. Such was the extent of the transfers from outside the district that some residents who owned businesses indicated in the Survey, that they themselves could have bought supplies from the large scale rice farmers for their own businesses. The large-scale rice farmers did however buy some food and very small amounts of supplies from the small businesses in the Biche / Plum Mitan district in order to temporarily take care of shortages.

pg. 29 **Value to the Macro-economy**

The effect of large-scale rice growing in Block B on the macro-economy of Trinidad and Tobago was insignificant. The total value of production was in the vicinity of $TT 12 million. In an economy with GDP that ranged from $TT 17,813.5 million to $TT 17,212.7 million (at current prices) from 1985 to 1989, this was less than 0.07% of GDP. The contribution of all Agriculture to GDP at this time ($465.2 million in 1989) was in the order of 2.7% meaning that the large-scale rice farmers were contributing about 2.37% of Agriculture's contribution to GDP.

Around 1987, when an expansion of rice production in Block B took place, rice was considered a major crop for food supplies for the nation. In a speech at a Seminar organised by the Faculty of Agriculture's Farm Management Information Systems (FMIS) Project, the then Minister of Agriculture [Myers] stated that his Ministry has "accorded rice the status of a priority commodity and to this end an inter-agency committee has been convened to co-ordinate, among other things, a strategy for the development of the rice industry."

Annually the rice farmers in Block B produced about 2850 tonnes of paddy rice. Production increased from 91.5 tonnes in 1986 to 4377.9 tonnes in 1992. This production converts to about 1852.5 tonnes of rice at a conversion rate of (paddy to rice) 0.65. This represented about 18% of the domestic production of rice, which in 1991 stood at 10,524 tonnes of rice. In 1991, the nation imported 21,676 tonnes of rice, 92% of these imports coming from the USA and the rest mainly from Guyana. Total consumption of rice was therefore 31,930 tonnes with domestic supply contributing 32% and the production of large-scale rice farmers contributed about 5.8% of this consumption.

Table 19. Domestic production of paddy in Trinidad and Tobago 1986 - 1992

YEAR	CARONI LTD.	LARGE FARMERS	SMALL FARMERS	TOTAL FARMERS	OVERALL TOTAL
1985	10	NA	NA	1500	1600
1986	39.2	91.5 (4.6%)*	1859.5	1951.5	1990.2
1987	1919.2	362.2 (4.7%)	3309.6	3672.3	5591
1988	1970	625.5 (14.4%)	3705.1	4330.5	6300
1989	3843.4	1339.2 (25.8%)	3860.9	5200.2	9043.5
1990	4774.8	1101.1 (11.9%)	8168.5	9269.1	14043.4
1991	5642	2096.9 (11.9%)	8452.5	10549.9	16190.5
1992	6418.2	4377.9 (28.3%)	11093.5	15471.9	21889.6
1993	4800	NA	NA	11100	15900
1994	4000	NA	NA	12500	16600
1995	3000	NA	NA	6000	9000

NA not available   *% of total farmer's production

pg. 30.

Long Term Economic Damage

Prior to large scale farming agricultural activity in Block B was 110 hectares out of 6000 hectares for Nariva Swamp. The percentage of the area affected was 1.8%. The social non-user value of $608,000,000 at 1.8% of the swamp = $10.9 million.

Large Scale Rice Growing

1,200 hectares or 18.7% plus previous agricultural activity displaced, or 1090 hectares Environmental damage = $110.5 million.

Optimal Resource Use Determination

Multi-criterion model provided feasible options for Nariva: Okro, Bodie, Pumpkin, Melon 672 hectares, Squash, Ecotourism 256 hectares

pg. VI.

The area of melon proposed, 672 hectares is greater than the actual estimated area. This shows that melon is the crop with the greatest potential for the Nariva Swamp. Rice is not included in the optimal solution, showing that while it is a swamp crop, the economics of its production in Trinidad does not justify its production in the Nariva Swamp. This result is consistent with a pattern of increased melon production and reduced rice production in the Swamp. An ecotourism activity is also included in the model, utlising an area of 256 hectares The total net revenue for this solution is approximately $15 million, which is greater than the estimated net revenue from crops of $8.2 million for small farmers in Block A and Kernahan.

Economic Impact of Large Scale Rice Growing in Block B

1. total acreage of large-scale rice farming in Block B - 950 hectares

total acreage farmed before large-scale rice farming in Block B - 101.25 hectares

2. total cost of inputs per annum for large-scale rice farming in Block B $8,779,900

3. total cost of inputs per annum for economic activities before large-scale rice farming in Block B was $567,609

4. the value of production per year for large scale rice farming in Block B was $11,172,000

5. the value of production per year from economic activities before large-scale rice farming in Block B was $846,646

6. The net revenue per year for large-scale rice farming in Block B was $2,392,100.

7. The net revenue per year from economic activities before large-scale rice farming in Block B was $279,037.

8. For large-scale rice production in Block B the net revenue after the overall subsidy is subtracted (Social Value of Production), is equal to:

Total Net Revenue - Subsidies = $2,392,100 - $6,641,863 = negative $4,249,763

9. Therefore while large scale rice farming in Block B gave private returns (net revenue) of $2,392,100 per year, the social value of this production was negative $4,249,763 because of the actual and implied subsidies received by the rice farmers.

10. The net revenue after overall subsidy (Social Value of Production) of agricultural activity prior to rice farming was $279,037 - $1781 = $277,256, where, $1781 represents the implied subsidy of using the land without payment of land rent to the State.

11. 1090 hectares of Nariva Swamp were permanently modified by large-scale rice growing causing permanent damage of $110.5 million.

It may be concluded that rice growing was not socially desirable as the previous economic activity. Thus large-scale rice growing in Block B had an overall negative impact on the nation (underlined in original).

pg. viii. Activity 4. Economic Impact of Feasible Options

The net revenue of the feasible options is $15.3 million, which is the sum of the net revenue from crops and ecotourism of $14.9 million, as well as $353,820 from fishing activity. The Social Value of Production is valued at $14.9 million and represents the Net Revenue less the amount of State subsidies envisaged. The State subsidies total $739,721, and are made up of:

(1) $20,721 representing the unpaid land rent on the 1178 hectares of land used. It is assumed in the model that the State programme of leasing land will be long delayed in implementation.

(2) $500,000 represents the annual value of the start up costs of $5 million necessary for the success of the ecotourism enterprise. It is assumed here that the investment is depreciated at a straight-line rate of 10%.

(3) $219,000 representing the annual cost of manned patrols necessary for the ecotourism enterprise.

The value of the employment generated is $4,737,500. This labour consists of:

-68 fishermen

-400 farmers who are assumed to farm half of their time. Thus their labour is considered equivalent to 200 full time persons.

-91 hired farm labourers. This figure is calculated from the hired labour required of the various crops.

-20 persons hired in the ecotourism enterprise comprising 10 tour guides from the communities of the Nariva Swamp, 6 guards to patrol the area to facilitate tourism and 4 tour operators. The full time employment is therefore 379 individuals, and the value of this labour is calculated as 379 persons * 50 weeks * 5 days/week * $50/day = $4,737,500.

The land values in the areas surrounding the Nariva Swamp are expected to gain in value because of the implementation of the feasible options. Similarly the surrounding community will benefit from the feasible options, especially the ecotourism enterprise. As stated earlier, this enterprise will employ at least 20 persons from the surrounding areas as tour guides and this will bring an additional income of $125,000 (10 persons * 501 weeks * 5 days * $50/day). The feasible options could form the basis of both a Management Plan for the Nariva Swamp as well as a Development Plan for the area.

Should we farm the Nariva Swamp ? V.C. Quesnel. 1972.

In September, 1966, at the invitation of the Government of Trinidad and Tobago, a Japanese team of experts arrived in Trinidad to undertake a survey of the Nariva Swamp with a view to reclaiming it for agricultural purposes. Two further visits and at least two reports followed this. Before this, in 1957, a Dutch team had surveyed the swamp with the same end in view. It is reasonable to conclude therefore that the Government sees the swamp as an undeveloped resource, which may be worth developing. Let us address ourselves therefore to the question, Should we farm the Nariva Swamp?

The Nariva area may be considered to be the triangular area of approximately 60,000 acres between the sea to the east, the Lower Manzanilla Road, the Plum Mitan and Cunapo Southern roads to the north and west and the Rio Claro Mayaro road to the south. Several rivers from the Central Range discharge into the low plain eventually overflowing their banks and joining to form a freshwater swamp of approximately 40,000 acres. From this the exit to the sea is via the Nariva River which after following a course approximately parallel to the coast for some 3 or 4 miles empties into the Atlantic about two thirds of the way down the eastern coast. The area actually under water varies considerably with the season but even during the dry season 10,500 acres always remain flooded.

Two soil types are represented in the area permanently under water - Nariva swamp clay and Macaw peaty clay. The former consists of 6" of black, humic clay overlying seven feet of a uniform dark grey, acid (pH 4 - 5), clay of butter-like consistency. The latter consists of at least seven feet of loose, dark brown, acid, humic clay or silty clay. The vegetation on the former is Cascadoux grass (*Leersia hexandra*) and on the latter a mixture of palms (*Roystonea oleracea*) ferns (*Acrostichum aureum*) and aroids (*Montrichardia arborescens*).

The area not permanently inundated consists mainly of two soil types, Bois Neuf clay and Navet clay. The former is about 5,000 acres in extent and consists of a topsoil of 3" of dark greyish brown, humic clay over deeper layers of brownish grey and purplish grey clay. The whole profile is very acid, (pH 4.0), but is well supplied with nitrogen and phosphorus. The vegetation is mainly Montrichardia and sedge (*Cyperus giganteus*). The Navet clay, which extends over about 29,000 acres consists of a thin (3") layer of brown clay with orange mottles. Below this again are layers of putty coloured and blue-grey clays. All layers are extremely acid (pH 3.5 - 4.5) but are well supplied with plant nutrients except calcium. The overlying vegetation is mainly forest in which crappo (*Carapa guianensis*) and spiny palms (*Bactris* spp.) predominate.

Although the margins of the swamp are already partly settled and cultivated the swamp itself is relatively inaccessible and therefore remains an important refuge for wild life. Wild game, monkeys, birds, snakes, butterflies and freshwater fish are still plentiful and some of these resources are already exploited. Wild game is hunted and approximately two hundred (200) people make a living off fishing the swamp, either for food or for aquarium fish.

In the period 1954 - 56 a Dutch team visited Trinidad and surveyed the Nariva Swamp for reclamation as part of a wider survey of all the swamp areas: Caroni, Laventille, Nariva, Oropouche and Fishing Pond. Their report published in 1957 contained the following conclusions:

"19. For the Nariva area the most likely development would be to penetrate the area gradually from the higher grounds to the west.

20. To be effective, improvement of local drainage will have to be combined with an extensive programme of river clearing and widening. These drainage works might require the construction of an intercepting canal around the swamp proper.

21. A detailed survey will have to provide the final answer to what extent the land now under forest could be converted to other uses.

22. If the economic aspects should rule out a general improvement, two polders with a total gross area of 4,600 acres could be developed in the more elevated flat lands of the herbaceous swamp. A serious drawback of this development would be that the area is situated in the middle of inaccessible swamplands, so that an assimilation with Trinidad community would be difficult to obtain.

23. As the quality of the soil is very likely to be very bad in the swamp proper, a detailed soil survey should precede any reclamation work in this area."

Costs for the reclamation of the whole area were not estimated except that they would be very high. The cost of the construction for the two polders of 4,600 total acreage was estimated at $2,030,000 i.e. $450 per acre. There was no estimate of maintenance costs.

Although the report dealt mainly with the engineering aspects of the work and gave details of the plans for drainage and irrigation of the polders other aspects were not ignored. For instance, the authors emphasized the need for soil studies to show whether or not the reclaimed land would be able to support and keep on supporting a profitable agriculture. They emphasized the many unknown economic aspects and they drew attention to the possible ecological side effects. They considered that the disturbance of the present equilibrium between river flow and wave action by removal of water from the swamp would lead to the formation of a sand bar across the mouth of the Nariva River.

But perhaps even more interesting are the general remarks in Chapter 19, 'Prospects for Agricultural Development in Trinidad'. Under the section Land Utilization the report states: 'the inclusion of this general section in the report is justified on the grounds that swamp reclamation presupposes a land shortage in Trinidad of a most desperate kind. The technical sections of the report emphasize the peculiarities of swamps, the high cost of reclamation and the maintenance of reclamation works and the extremely difficult agriculture conditions that are likely to be encountered in the reclaimed areas. Even if every square mile of the present agricultural land of the island were cultivated at maximum intensity there would still be areas available for development more suitable than the swamps. For instance, the development of El Tucuche by proper soil conservation and improved communications would be cheaper, acre for acre, than any swamp scheme; the climatic and soil conditions on that mountain (as far as they are known) are likely to be more amenable to agricultural development that the swamps'.

'In spite of the popular demand for more agricultural land there is at the present time no land shortage in Trinidad'.
The report goes on to support this assertion by quoting a survey, which showed that in an area roughly co-extensive with Caroni County exclusive of the swamp, 52% of the land was uncultivated. Of the 52%, 64 was in high bush, 22% in grass that was sparingly grazed and the remainder was in low scrub. The report states bluntly that the demands for land are 'indicative of poor standards of farming rather than an absolute shortage of land'.
The report next examines two possible lines of development, the revival of the cocoa industry and small farming. It states baldly 'In this industry, as with most other agriculture in Trinidad, land is not the problem; the problem is lack of capital and management'. The revival of the cocoa industry may not in 1972 seem quite the attractive proposition it did in 1957 but it is still worth considering.

The case for small farming is vigorously argued and the possibilities emphasized though this development is considered to be no easier and certainly slower than the revival of cocoa. Rice is seen as having no place in this development for the following reasons;
1. It is highly seasonal in its labour demands so that while placing a limit on the area that can be cultivated by a family it does not provide year-round occupation.
2. Other enterprises are not easily combined with it.
3. There is little scope for increasing earnings by mechanisation or other techniques.

4. It is a low output crop earning only $200 per acre (1959) for a heavy labour input on expensively developed land.

'It is no wonder therefore that there is no possibility in producing rice in Trinidad competitively for export ..... The popularity of rice schemes in policy making circles is due to the fact that rice is the basic food of virtually the whole population. A greater production of the most basic requirement is often assumed to be an important economic objective without much thought being given to the proposition. However, Trinidad is exceptionally well situated to engage in international trade and the food supplied is in fact imported from every corner of the globe. She is then placed in a position to export products most urgently needed by other countries and for which they are prepared to pay ...... The objective of Trinidad as with any other country possessing economic ambitions is to increase productivity per head of population. One certain method of not achieving this is by ignoring her greatest natural advantage that allow here to participate in international trade and developing xenomaniac policies of self-subsistence'.

The Japanese team that followed ten (10) years later went through the same exercise of surveying the swamp, outlining the problems and providing suggested solutions. They produced a plan for draining the whole swamp, not just two polders, giving all the engineering features. The cut-off canal, which the Dutch had proposed earlier as an optional feature, became a key feature of their plan. According to newspaper reports the Japanese estimated a cost of $56,000,000 for the reclamation of the whole swamp exclusively of an area of 6,000 acres, which would remain permanently under water. This works out at $1,650 per acre for 34,000 acres.

The normal cost of clearing forest land and preparing it for planting was, in 1969, about $250 per acre - less than one sixth of the cost of reclaiming the swamp. In this then the Japanese bear out the Dutch; the cost of reclaiming swampland is excessively high when compared with bringing other land into production. Had the country developed in the meantime to such an extent that other usable land had already been used ? We just have to look around us to answer that question in the negative but available statistics support our intuitive answer. According to reports of the Central Statistical Office, in 1959 there were 124,650 acres of abandoned land, secondary growth or lastro and 99,450 acres of semi-derelict land under shifting cultivation. In 1963, the latest figures available, there were 201,650 acres under tree crops and 116,500 acres in secondary growth or lastro. Since part of the area under tree crops is surely inadequately farmed or almost abandoned the area of usable land - badly cultivated or uncultivated but once cultivated - is hardly different from the 1959 figure. Since 1963, the crown lands scheme has brought under cultivation only about

10,000 acres. Thus, now as in 1957, there is no land shortage. There are well over 100,000 acres of cultivated land, which could be brought into production at a small fraction of the cost of reclaiming the swamp. As was mentioned earlier most of the land, which would be made available for agriculture by draining the Nariva swamp, is of the Navet clay soil type. For crops other than rice this would require intensive improvement and the cost involved would be additional to the cost of reclamation and a continuing added cost if productivity is to be maintained. The 100,000 acres of other available land is generally of a rather poor soil type but not so bad as that of Navet clay. Therefore improvement would be less costly than the improvement required for Navet clay.

Other aspects of cost that are not so obvious must be considered. If the swamp were drained a sand bar would develop across the mouth of the Nariva River as already pointed out, but, more important, salt water would be almost certain to seep through the sandy Cocal and into the low lying parts of the drained swamp. Since drying swamplands always shrink it would cause no surprise if the land level in the drained area fell below sea level and contributed to the inward flow of seawater. This ingress of seawater would damage the coconut estate along the coast and the cost of compensation would add another few million dollars to the bill. Further in the parts of the swamp that would remain under water, the water would become brackish and salt would probably move into the cultivated areas creating problems for the agriculturist and increasing the cost of the operations.

By opening up the area to agriculture and changing the ecological conditions the wild life will be greatly affected. Some animals would die out, some would move away and try to establish themselves elsewhere, and others might disperse temporarily only to return as pests feeding on the crops that were planted. It is impossible to foresee in detail the changes that would occur but profound changes there would be. Equally too, it is impossible to forecast the effect if any on the offshore fisheries from disturbance of run off and from pollution with agricultural chemicals.

To the question, should we farm the Nariva swamp? the answer must be NO; not in my lifetime anyway. The answer may be different in one hundred years' time but a more efficient agriculture must expand and occupy profitably all the more accessible land before this question need be considered again.

Final report - EIA

FINAL REPORT - EIA OF THE AGRICULTURAL ACTIVITIES WITHIN THE
BICHE BOIS NEUF AREA (BLOCK B)
Executive Summary

The Institute of Marine Affairs (IMA) was contracted by the Government of Trinidad
and Tobago, through the Ministry of Agriculture, Land and Marine Resources
(MALMR), to conduct an Environment Impact Assessment (EIA) of agricultural
activities in the Biche Bois Neuf Area (Block B) of the Nariva Swamp and their impacts
(ecological, social and economic) on the entire wetland.

The Nariva Swamp is the largest and most diverse wetland ecosystem in
Trinidad and Tobago. It is located on the east coast of Trinidad....covering an area of
approximately 6,000 hectares The diversity of plants and animals within the system is
extremely high, and it is the habitat of a number of highly sensitive plants and animals.

The Environment Impact Assessment (EIA) for the Block B area of the Nariva
Swamp is the third document submitted to the Monitoring Committee of the Ministry
of Agriculture, Land and Marine Resources. It is based on data collected from
September 1997 to May 1998 on all aspects of the environment of Nariva Swamp; the
impacts of large-scale rice farming in Block B have been identified, and mitigatory
recommendations have been provided. Impacts were identified for three phases;
namely (i) site modification (ii) agricultural operations and (iii) post-rice farming.

The results of legal studies indicated that the farmers occupied the lands illegally,
but that the laws and policies governing the environment and its use are unclear. These
need to be clarified, and brought into accordance with international protocols and
conventions, especially with respect to habitat protection.

The hydrogeological studies indicated that the agricultural activities of the large-
scale rice farmers altered the seasonal distribution of water within the swamp, resulting
in reduction of ground water levels in Block B and increased drying out of regions of
the swamp during the dry season. The possibility of salt water intrusion into the swamp
also increased. Rice agronomic practices should pursue an Integrated Crop
Management (ICM) approach using zero pesticide and fertiliser inputs.

The water and sediment study indicated high levels of DDE (a breakdown
product of DDT), and high ammonia levels at the Jagroma River and the Petit Poole
Canal. Copper level in the water and soils of Blocks A and B were similar. The high

level of nutrients from fertilisers could lead to eutrophication of the waterways if rice farming is resumed in the way it was in the past. The ecological study revealed decreases in the abundance and diversity of waterfowl, and overall area of vegetative ecotypes. There was also a reduction in the water supply to the manatee ponds, which may have reduced the range of this endangered species within the swamp. The causes of these were attributed to activities associated with large-scale rice farming. The aquatic fauna would have suffered from excessive drying out of habitats, mechanical damage from equipment, burning operations and loss of habitat. However, the use of fertilisers would have increased the primary productivity of the system, and the canals and drains would have provided alternative habitats for the fauna. As far as possible, habitat restoration in areas surrounding Block B should be attempted if rice farming is to be resumed. In the absence of rice farming, habitats should be restored to their natural state as far as possible.

The socio-economic study indicated conflicts between the large-scale farmers and the communities surrounding the swamp. These arose because of restrictions on access to areas of Block B and reduced benefits to the local community. There was also conflict within the large-scale rice farming community. The study suggests methods, such as security of land tenure for small farmers in Block A, to help alleviate some of these conflicts.

The economic study indicated that the subsidies on the rice produced in Block B and the non-internalisation of environmental costs were responsible for the profits of the farmers. The net revenue per year from economic activities in Block B increased from TT$279,037 (before large-scale rice farming) to TT$2,392,100. However, since state subsidies in Block B increased from TT$1718 to TT$6,641,863, the social cost of production was -TT$4,249,763 because of actual and implied subsidies. In addition, the activity contributed only marginally to the macroeconomy, amounting to about 0.07% of country GDP or about 2,37% of agriculture's contribution to GDP.

The rice farming activities only marginally improved employment opportunities in the local communities. It is suggested that the social costs incurred by the rice farming activities be borne by the farmers in order to allow them to make decisions, which reflect the true cost of rice farming.

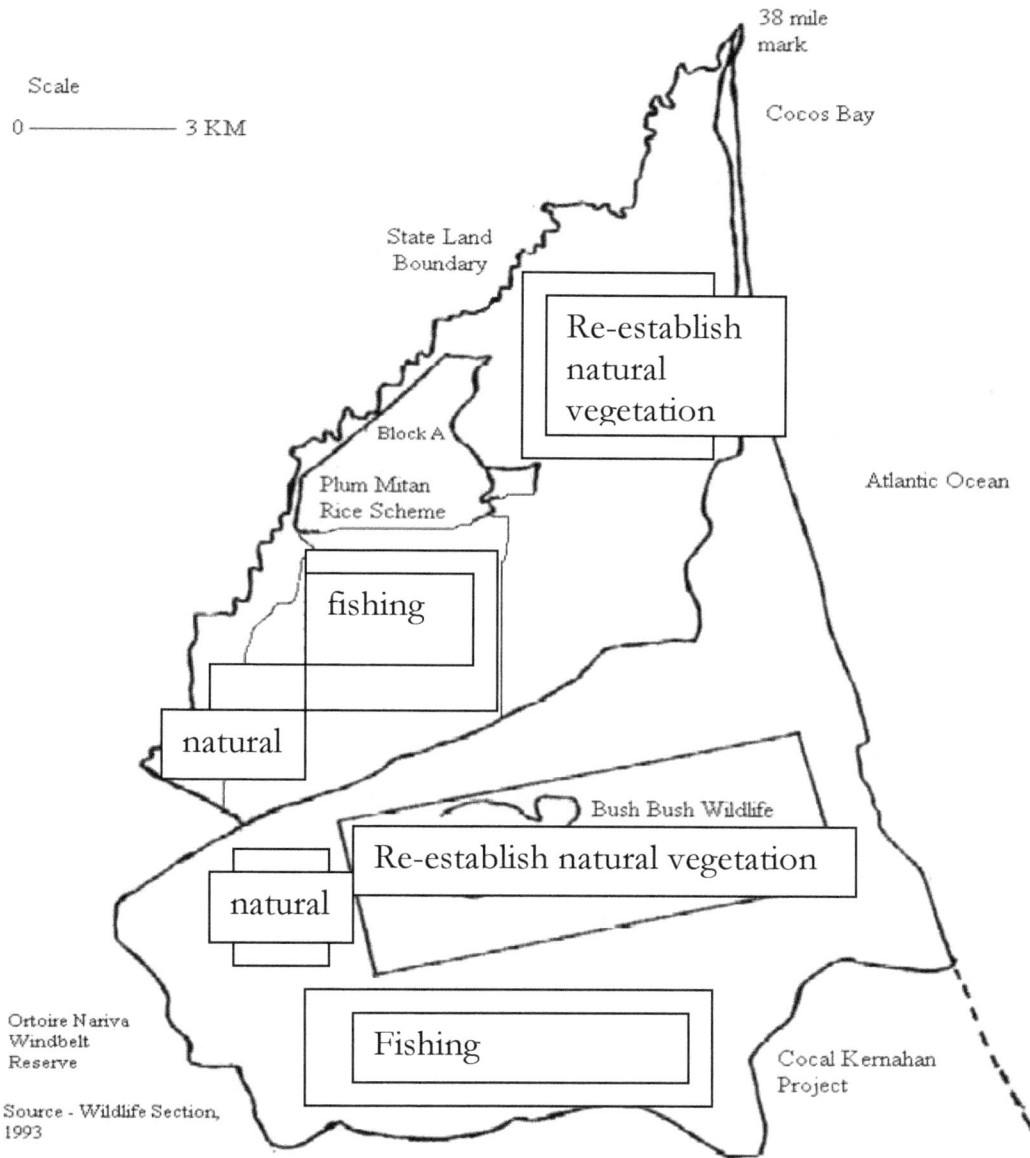

Fig 5. Management of the Nariva Swamp proposed by IMA 1999

National policy on wetland conservation

NATIONAL POLICY ON WETLAND CONSERVATION. TRINIDAD AND TOBAGO. DRAFT. PREPARED BY THE NATIONAL WETLAND COMMITTEE. JAN 16, 1996.
APPENDIX 2. RELEVANT LEGAL AND INSTITUTIONAL FRAMEWORK.
BACKGROUND TO POLICY

There is no written Government policy with regard to wetlands in Trinidad and Tobago. The only clear statements of policy are the facts that Trinidad and Tobago became a Contracting Party to the RAMSAR Convention in December 1992, with effect from April 1993, that Nariva Swamp was designated for inclusion in the RAMSAR List of Wetlands of International Importance, and the appointment of the National Wetland Committe in 1995.

Otherwise policy and intentions must be inferred from political manifestos, draft legislation, Ministerial speeches, and recent Government actions.

The election manifesto of the United National Congress (1995) refers to concerns for natural resources as a crisis. It refers to "The continued degradation of our physical environment and the wasting of our natural resources continue to increase ---" and implies that this has been a result of a lack of caring in policy implementation, and a tendency to " -- 'cook deals' which are inimical to our society."

It states an intention to focus on policies and programmes to target, amongst other factors, "Improvement of the physical and natural environment to support sustainable development for current and future generations."

Tourism is important, including "--- the development of inland and marine parks, nature trails, inland and coastal aqua-sports enclaves and resorts -- " for ecotourism. The section on Environment states "Proper management of our natural resources and environment is absolutely essential --" and pledges the UNC to "--- develop attitudes which will encourage sustainable utilization --." It relies on the Environment Management Authority "-- to play a key role in formulating policy, regulation and public awareness on environmental issues."

There is however no policy statement on wetlands or any other aspect of Forestry Division's mandate.

Other indications of policy on wetlands are to be found in current draft Forest Resources and National Parks legislation, and the Bucoo Reef Management Plan, which incorporates management of the reef and part of the wetland and sea grass area. However these have not yet become firm reality.

Appendix 2: Trinidad and Tobago's agricultural policies as they relate to rice and the Nariva Swamp in chronological order

RICE REPORT 1

A SURVEY OF THE RICE INDUSTRY. STATISTICAL STUDIES AND PAPERS NO. 2. PRELIMINARY REPORT ISSUED JOINTLY BY THE RICE DIVISION OF THE DEPARTMENT OF AGRICULTURE AND THE CENTRAL STATISTICAL OFFICE. AUGUST 1953. H.J. STEER AND E.G. BENSON

pg. 2. The expansion of local production has not kept pace with the increases in the population. Today rice is scarce; since 1964 it has been necessary to ration imported supplies. For these reasons the Government of Trinidad has, for some time past, been anxious to encourage the expansion of the rice industry.

<u>Attempts to Increase Rice Production</u>

Attempts to drain the Caroni Swamp had been made by private enterprise as far back as 1920. For financial and other reasons such attempts failed. During the years of the second world war, a scheme for irrigating some 2,200 acres of land at Bejucal (a portion of the Caroni Swamp) was completed by the Works and Hydraulics Department at a capital cost of $978,758 and an annual maintenance cost of $27,500. This is now a declared drainage area, zoned for the production of paddy and controlled by the Works and Hydraulics Department. Improvements were also started in two neighbouring small rice areas of El Socorro and St. Augustine at capital costs of $28,082 and $27,097 respectively. In addition, the Works and Hydraulics Department maintains an inadequate drainage system in the Oropouche Lagoon at an annual cost of $46,000.

In February 1949, Government appointed an ad hoc Committee with the following terms of reference :-

" To consider in the light of all relevant factors, - agricultural, economic, financial, etc., -of which the Committee may inform itself or which may be brought to its notice in evidence and to recommend what steps should be taken to promote increased production of rice in the Colony."

The findings of this Committee are reported in Council Paper No. 2 of 1950.

The accepted recommendations are summarised below.

a. That Government should recognize the importance to the Colony of the rice industry and should adopt a strong progressive policy towards it.
b. That all price controls on locally grown rice should be removed.
c. That no large project should be tackled at present, but instead there should be a gradual and steady expansion of small schemes, particularly in areas of large population.
d. That publicity should be given to methods of increasing average production, through the provision of better seed, and the introduction of new varieties, as soon as these have been thoroughly tested by the Department of Agriculture.
e. That Government should appoint a Rice Officer to the Department of Agriculture, whose duties should be confined to the extension of rice growing.
f. That Standing Rice Committee should be appointed to advise and guide the future of the industry.

All of these accepted recommendations operate today. Towards the end of 1950 the Rice Officer was appointed to the Agricultural Department.

pg. 11. Economic and Sociological Survey

A survey was undertaken to obtain up-to-date and accurate information on conditions and practices from a few randomly selected farms. Although restricted to farms in four rice areas -Caroni, Oropouche, Fishing Pond, and Plum Mitan - a great deal of detailed information was collected from each farm and it is believed that the data collected will be useful for some time for general studies of the rice industry in the Colony.
Each farmer was visited on a number of occasions between June 1951 and January 1952.

Of the acreage farmed 254.06 acres only (i.e. 42%) were padi land. The proportion of the total farmed area devoted to rice was greatest in the Caroni district where it reached 67%, and lowest, 12% in Plum Mitan.

Table 20. Economic and sociological survey (produced from data on pg. 11).

	Selection of sample of farmers	Acres farmed	Avg. size of farm	Avg. area of rice/farm
Caroni	22	135.50	6.15	4.10
Oropouche	60	308.31	5.14	2.29
Fishing Pond	12	106.50	9.7	1.73
Plum Mitan	11	59.00	4.91	0.58

Table 21. Size of farms showing areas devote to padi and other uses. Plum Mitan

Size of farms (acres)	No. of farms	Area	No. of separate parcels	Av. size of parcel
<1	3	1.50	3	0.50
1 – 2	1	1.50	2	0.75
2 – 3	1	2.00	1	2.00
3 – 4	1	3.50	2	1.75
4 – 5	-	-	-	-
5 – 10	-	-	-	-
10 – 20	3	41.50	4	10.37
>20	2	56.50	2	28.25
TOTALS	11	106.50	14	7.61
% of total area of farmed land	-	-	-	-
avg. per farm	-	9.7	-	-

Table 22. Riceland

	AREA	No. of separate fields	Avg. size of field	Permanent Crops	Other crops
< 1	1.50	3	0.50		
1 – 2	1.50	2	0.75		
2 – 3	2.00	1	2.00		
3 – 4	1.00	1	1.00	2.50	
4 – 5	-	-	-	-	
5 – 10	-	-	-	-	
10 - 20	9.50	3	3.17	28.00	4.00
> 20	3.50	2	1.75	53.00	
TOTALS	19.00	12	1.58	83.50	
%	18%	-	-	78%	
Avg. per farm	1.73	-	-		

Table 23. The conditions of tenure of land in Plum Mitan

Land owned	Land owned and sublet	Land owned and farmed	Land rented	Land rented and sublet	Land rented and farmed by first renter	Total land farmed by farmers in sample	% owned and farmed (acres)
a	B	a-b	c	d	c-d	(a-b)+(c-d)	
99.50	3.00	96.50	10.00	0.00	10.00	106.50	91.00

RICE REPORT 2

PEASANT FARMING IN THE BEJUCAL AREA OF TRINIDAD. A.L. JOLLY. TROPICAL AGRICULTURE VOL. XX11. NO. 5. 1945

pg. 83.

Bejucal remained practically uncultivated until 1895 when parcels were for the first time allotted to East Indian labourers who wished to remain in the island on the completion of their indentured service. About seven-eights of the area was distributed to East Indians from 1895 to 1907 ; the usual grant consisted of about 3 acres.

pg. 85.

Table 24 gives a comparison of costs and income for the three major crops. It is evident that high income per acre and per man-day was earned from provisions in spite of high costs being incurred. Rice was the second most costly crop but yielded relatively low net income. Cane was an extensive crop, low costs and low income per acre being characteristic; it is to be noted, however, that the earnings per man-day were considerably higher for cane than for rice.

Table 24. Income and costs per acre for three crops in the Bejucal Area

ACREAGE	CANE	RICE	PROVISIONS
($ per Acre)	438	251	225
Income	60	94	174
Total Labour (ex family labour)	15	39	25
Manure	2	-	3
Rent*	3	5	4
Seed	-	4	28
Total Cost	20	48	60
Net income	40	46	114
Family Man-days available per acre	35	63	65
Net Income per Man-day available	$1.14	$0.72	$1.75

* Land rented for $8 - $10 per acre but all land was not, of course, rented: 40%, 47% respectively of the Cane, Rice and Provision land was rented.
pg. 85.

The range in net income of the three crops is compared in Table 25. It can be seen that rice and provisions gave very variable results, provisions rather more so than rice. The income from cane, on the other hand, showed comparatively little variation, nearly two-thirds of the acreage being cultivated at a profit of $0 - 50 per acre. Cane was therefore the safest crop; provisions offered the possibility of very high profits but entailed considerable uncertainty ; rice offered almost equal uncertainty and no prospect of high profit.

Table 25. Profitability of three crops per acre in the Bejucal Area

	CANE	CANE	RICE	RICE	PROVSIONS	PROVISIONS
	ACRES	%	ACRES	%	ACRES	%
LOSSES						
-$47 - $25	8	2	1	-	-	-
-$24 - $0	9	2	19	8	3	1
PROFITS						
$0 - $24	161	37	50	20	6	3
$25 - $49	97	22	74	29	18	8
$50 - $74	99	23	55	22	29	13
$75 - $99	37	8	32	13	44	20
$100 - $124	15	3	18	7	42	19
$125 - $149	11	3	2	1	35	15
$150 AND OVER	1	-	-	-	48	21
TOTAL	438	100	251	100	225	100

pg. 86. Rice cultivation. The relationship between profits and yields for rice were found to be the reverse of that for cane. With rice, profits were variable but yield was remarkably constant. Although rice is agriculturally the most difficult of the three crops, two-thirds of the acreage yielded between 2,000 and 3,000 lbs. paddy per acre. This small variation is undoubtedly due to the peasants' anxiety to avoid a crop failure : no

complete failures were recorded and only one-fifth of the acreage yielded less than 1,500 lbs. per acre.

pg. 87. The peasant's concern over his rice crop is understandable when it is realised that 70 per cent of the crop is consumed in households and that this food (valued at 3.5 c. per lb. paddy) makes up one-quarter of the total food expenditure. These facts explain why peasants willingly continue rice cultivation for a relatively low return of only 72 cents per man-day available.

pg.89. Part of the wasteful expenditure on rice cultivation is due to the peasant's anxiety to obtain an ample food supply from his acre or so of the crop and part is no doubt due to his inherent liking for, and pride in, the crop that figures so largely in his daily meals. Indeed, rice growing appears to be much more a part of the peasants' family life than of his business activities as a farmer.

The character of the rice crop as shown by the survey raises the whole question of whether it is feasible in Trinidad to obtain an appreciable surplus of rice at reasonable prices from peasant production. Under present methods of cultivation rice would have to sell at very high prices (at least 7 cents per lb. paddy off the holding) for peasants to obtain earnings comparable with other crops. On the other hand, cheapening of costs could only be achieved by destroying the essentially "family" nature of the crop. Costs could be cheapened by co-operative cultivation of areas considerably larger than the one or two acres of the individual peasant, but such co-operation would destroy the peasant's independence as a provider for himself and his family.

The recommendation to be made about rice is therefore that if the policy is to obtain a supply for urban consumption at reasonable prices, production from estates rather than from peasants appears to be more likely to attain the object. If the more important object is to develop a contented and self reliant peasantry, the policy most likely to succeed with East Indians is that of making rice lands available to them.

In view of the pressure exerted by farmers on the Government for land to be used for Agriculture, it seems that every effort should be made to improve the access facilities, and the drainage if immediately feasible, on the lands that are now occupied by both tenants and squatters. These occupiers should be regularised and placed on their holdings along with other farmers who may desire lands in these areas.

SUMMARY OF RECOMMENDATIONS

1. Government should establish a Unit to collect and study the necessary feasibility data for the overall development of the Nariva Swamp. A small station should be set up in the area by the Ministry of Agriculture and Ministry of Works to collect hydrologic, physiographic and crop data, as well as a study of the soils and the soil-water relationships of the area.

5. We recommend that pending an integral study of the Swamp in its hydrologic and social and economic aspects, that the following limited programme be carried out:

(a) construction of an unsurfaced access road (cost $22,000) between the private coconut plantations and the area farmed by the small holders, with connections to the Manzanilla Road at half mile intervals.

(b) A programme of river clearing be undertaken by ditch blasting to relieve flooding in the hinterland flats (cost $40,000). Alter the Jagroma Cut to allow the river to contribute to irrigation.

(c) Leveling of the entire area and the installation of a sluice gate to prevent the intrusion of salt water ($60,000).

(d) The construction of fish ponds in the perennially water logged area. This could be a big economic outlet for the area.

(e) Extension of the Plum Mitan scheme ($100,000). The occupied areas of the Swamp should be surveyed and laid out into 5, 10 and 20 acre blocks and these should be released to the occupiers who would then be regularised tenants.

(f) Construction of an all weather road from the Cascadoux Trace off the Manzanilla Road to the Cunapo Southern Road via the Biche Ortoire Road ($120,000).

CONCLUSION

The effect of such a programme should be the temporary alleviation of floods, an increase in employment and incomes as well as an increase in the area harvested.

RICE REPORT 4

DRAFT SECOND FIVE - YEAR PLAN 1964 - 1968. NATIONAL PLANNING COMMISSION.

NATIONAL PLANNING COMMISSION: Dr. Eric Williams, Mr. Arthur, N. Robinson, Mr. John O'Halloran, Mr. Robert Wallace, Mr. Lionel Robinson, Mr. Louis Alan Reece, Mr. Jack Harewood, Mrs. Patricia Robinson, Mr. David Weintraub, Mr. William Demas

Government Printery, Trinidad and Tobago, 1963. Chapter XIV pgs. 173, 179, 201..203

The food import bill is not only high but growing and is now in the vicinity of the sum of $70m. per annum. A dominant objective of policy must therefore be to reduce the share of imports in total food consumption in order to achieve a greater degree of self-sufficiency and to protect the balance of payments. The achievement of the goals of greater self-sufficiency in food with a consequent reduction in the share of imports in food consumption, and the dampening down of the incipient inflationary pressure on food prices, depend to a very great extent over the plan period on the small and medium sized farmer. The aim over the plan period, is therefore, to establish the basis for a productive small and medium farm system geared to produce increasing quantities of milk, eggs, poultry, green vegetables, root crops, pork and pulses for the local market and in some instances for export in processed form. The establishing of such a system should do much to encourage existing small farmers to stay on the land and make use of the opportunities that exist in farming.

Rice constitutes a large part of the diet of most of the population. While annual per capita consumption has risen from approximately 86 pounds in 1955 to about 158 pounds in the 1960s. Local production had declined from 12,000 tons in 1952 to 10,000 tons in 1961. The contribution of local production to total supply has declined to 30 per cent. Rice is grown as a subsistence or subsidiary crop. Since 1952 the acreage under rice has declined from 18,000 acres to 15,000 acres in 1961. Land has been switched to the more profitable eddoes and sugar, the latter due to the expectation of a good quota on the American market.

Price-wise local growers cannot compete with British Guiana. As far as quality is concerned, Trinidad rice is not in the forefront. Greater rice production locally would call for substantial capital investment for reclamation of swamp areas, for modernisation of the industry by the provision of drying and milling facilities, and for some degree of mechanisation and irrigation. The question therefore, resolves itself into whenever the use of more land and capital for the purpose of rice cultivation would constitute the best use of these resources when it is considered that there are other sectors in agriculture where returns are likely to be greater. Thus the value of alternative production foregone by producing the crop must be closely considered before the adoption of any schemes designed to promote self-sufficiency over the next five years, especially when there are good prospects of purchasing large amounts of rice at cheap prices from several sources. To admit this however is not to ignore the possibilities of encouraging the expansion of rice production in specific areas, particularly through the undertaking of limited drainage works and also perhaps through the provision of funds for the establishment of a rice-mill in the County of Caroni as one of the Agricultural Development Board projects.

pg. 186. Land settlement and use of marginal areas

One major project, the Oropouche Drainage Scheme, should lead to increased production on a considerable acreage in the South. Attention is also being given to the Nariva Swamp area in an effort to ascertain its potential for development.

RICE REPORT 5

WHITE PAPER ON AGRICULTURE, DECEMBER 1978. MINISTRY OF AGRICULTURE, LANDS AND FISHERIES. Government Printery, 1979.

2.3.5 pg. 8. Physical infrastructure

The provision of adequate physical infrastructure was designed to make significant impact in raising production and productivity levels. Major improvements were made in:

(ii) Land improvement - drainage and irrigation works in the Caroni and Nariva Swamps and the Oropouche Lagoon have increased the cultivable acreage under rice, vegetables and food crops.

pg. 10. Domestic agriculture. Significant increases were experienced in rice...156%. Despite overall increases in domestic production, Trinidad and Tobago continues to be a food-deficit country.

pg. 19.. 3.2 Development of Sub-Sectoral plans

National programmes have recently been or are being developed in relation to:

(c) Rice. The Rice Mill is in operation. The assured outlet provided, together with improvements in the physical infrastructure in rice producing areas and the provision of an incentive price will contribute significantly to increased domestic production of rice.

3.3 Expansion of the land resources base

Major efforts are being made related to increasing the available land resource base for expanded agricultural production. These include:

(1) Reclamation Of Swamp Areas

Investigative studies are being undertaken on the Nariva Swamp with a view to expanding the arable land base. A feasibility study on the Oropouche Lagoon has already been completed with financial assistance from the European Economic Commission. The implementation phase of this latter project is soon to be started. Both these projects also have implications for improvements in fisheries (fresh water species) and conservation of wildlife.

pg. 22. Despite serious efforts at reorganising the agricultural sector, and mainly because of constraints, there was no significant response in meeting either the increasing demand for food staples in the country or the expanded quotas for export crops on world markets. As a result of the experience gained in developing and implementing programmes and projects emanating from these plans, and because of the necessity to treat with the issues affecting agricultural development in the country today, it is perhaps both prudent and timely to redefine the problem and restate the objectives of agricultural policy.

pg. 23. The specific objectives of agricultural policy are outlined :-

1. to increase the production of food (including fish) in order to achieve the greatest measure of self-sufficiency and a consequent reduction of the proportion of imports in food consumption;

2. to ensure the production and distribution of foods of high nutritional value at reasonable consumer prices thereby reducing the incidence of malnutrition in the population;

3. to promote greater utilization of local foods;

4. to raise productivity and income levels in the agricultural (including fisheries and forestry) sector;

5. to ensure security in food supplies;

6. to promote the rational expansion of the forest and wildlife resources; and to maintain and increase future timber supplies by undertaking suitable regeneration methods after exploitation;

7. to stimulate employment through creation of greater linkages between agriculture (including fisheries and forestry) and industry and tourism;

8. to promote the development of rural communities by stimulating the growth of a vibrant agricultural sector;

9. to increase output from the traditional export agricultural sector through use of yield increasing technology on existing or reduced acreages;

10. to promote proper land use and natural resource conservation measures;

11. to promote the development of non-traditional export agricultural commodities;

12. to effect savings in foreign exchange by reducing imports.

pg. 25. The concern about the need to increase domestic agricultural production derives from the evidence of a growing food import bill, which in 1977 was approximately $366 million, up by 14 per cent over the 1976 figure of $321 million.

pg. 28. The principal components of the cereal imports are wheat based products and rice. The strategy is to reduce total wheat imports in current consumption to 62%. The deficit will be met by the expansion of domestic production of rice.

RICE REPORT 6

DRAFT ESTIMATE 1984 RECURRENT EXPENDITURE RICE
MAINTENANCE PROGRAMME. AGRICULTURAL ENGINEERING AND
DEVELOPMENT DIVISION. MINISTRY OF AGRICULTURE, LANDS AND
FOOD PRODUCTION. TRINIDAD, JULY 1983

Introduction

The Agricultural Engineering and Development Division implements the Soil and Water Management Programme in rice-producing areas of the Country on behalf of the Extension Division of the Ministry of Agriculture, Lands and Food Production. This is essentially a maintenance programme for rice areas with major thrust on maintenance of water courses as well as drainage and irrigation systems. The maintenance of access roads and bridges in rice areas also forms an integral part of this programme in an attempt to provide better access to rice growing areas and thereby encourage farmers to grow more rice. Specific work programmes for Caroni, Penal, Superville, Kernahan and Plum Mitan have been developed by the Drainage and Irrigation Section of the Division.

The Draft Estimates for the Rice Maintenance programme includes $3,752,238.67 for Personnel Expenditure and $173,560 for Goods and Services.

Table 26. 1984 Rice projects summary of wages

PROJECTS	WAGES
CARONI	296,603.20
PENAL	586,398.60
SUPERVILLE	363,534.60
KERNAHAN	437,564.40
PLUM MITAN I	854,320.60
PLUM MITAN II	530,709.40
TOTAL	3,069,130.80

RICE REPORT 7. NO NAME 3. LOCAL RICE PRODUCTION

LARGE FARMERS

There are only four large farmers which presently cultivate an acreage of 2,700 acres among themselves. Two of these farmers own and cultivate 2,500 acres of rice land using a fully mechanised system while the other two own and cultivate 1,200 acres using partial mechanisation. The production of paddy for the last three years follows:

	LB.
1986	201,209
1987	796,824
1988	1,435,408

SMALL FARMERS

Rice production by small farmers is constrained by the large number of varieties and excess moisture content of the paddy delivered to the mill. As a result, post harvest losses are high, the milling out-turn is sub-optimal and the percentage of brokens correspondingly high. These factors have conspired to limit the financial viability of local rice milling operations. This has increased the attractiveness of rice importation in bulk for local packaging.

Greater self-sufficiency in rice production could be gained through:

(i) increasing the total acreages under rice;

(ii) raising crop yields;

(iii) improving post harvest handling, grading, drying, and milling operations.

As it is the small farmers yield per acre is presently higher than Caroni and the large farmers although a much lower grade of paddy with a higher moisture content is produced.

GOVERNMENT'S CONTRIBUTION/ROLE WITH RESPECT TO THE INFRASTRUCTURE FOR RICE PRODUCTION

In the National Agricultural Development Plan (1988 - 1992), the strategy for the further development of the rice industry was outlined as being designed to:

(i) increase the total area under rice;

(ii) raise crop yields;

(iii) promote vertical integration of the rice industry.

In addition, it is stated there that ."..the critical factor in expanding the rice areas would be the development of irrigation and drainage facilities", and the Plan goes on to identify the Plum Mitan, Caroni and Oropouche areas as being earmarked for the major thrust in this regard.

THE MINISTRY OF FOOD PRODUCTION AND MARINE EXPLOITATION (MFP&ME)

The reconstruction of access roads on private rice-growing lands has been minimal over the years and was usually done in an ad-hoc response to representations made by industrial farmers or their representatives. The Oropouche, Caroni and Kernahan areas have benefited most from these efforts. On State lands, the Plum Mitan Rice and Food Crop Project, has traditionally been specially selected for access road development. At present, the 480 hectare Plum Mitan project has in place approximately 50% of the roads which will be required for full development of these lands which the state in 1987 began to tenant with selected farmers. The Kernahan rice area in Nariva/Mayaro has in recent years, suffered in production levels due in part to the lack of development of access roads.

On the large state projects, Plum Mitan has again been selected for access road and other development in 1989, but it is unlikely that the planners' targets will be achieved, for reasons given below. The Plan recognises the potential of the Plum Mitan project for increased rice production and has assigned it a high priority with the hope that it will ."..raise coverage of domestic demand by local supply from 10 to 15%..."

There exists detailed plans for all aspects of the further development of the Plum Mitan area and the EEC has been approached for funding. Substantial access road (+ other) development is also planned for the Kernahan rice growing area. All of these projects will call for megadollars, so that what is really achieved in the short/medium run, will depend on the scale of (external) funding which becomes available.

APPENDIX 4: LOCAL RICE INDUSTRY. THE SETTING UP OF A BODY TO MONITOR AND REGULATE THE INDUSTRY

RATIONALE

" Improvement in sectoral performance should not be interpreted as substantially expanding agriculture's position in the national economy, rather it must be considered in terms of rationalizing production, improving incomes and conditions of tenure and generally of strengthening the economic foundations of the sector so that it becomes more attractive to both male and female participants and capable of existing without the large government subsidies historically provided." MISSION REPORT - FAO-MAY 1989

RICE REPORT 8   NATIONAL PLANNING COMMISSION

NATIONAL AGRICULTURAL DEVELOPMENT PLAN 1989 – 1995, OCTOBER 1988   SUMMARY OF PROPOSALS

4.3.7.4 STRATEGIES FOR DEVELOPMENT   pg. 32.

4.3.8 Rice

The importation of cereals and cereal preparations approximates 25% of the annual food import bill with a value of TT$240m. This food group includes wheat and rice which are major staples in the diet of the nation.

4.3.8.2. CONSTRAINTS ON PRODUCTION

Paddy production in Trinidad and Tobago has generally been at the subsistence level, with total production supplying about 5% of domestic demand. Production has been carried out on small holdings estimated at 1337 hectares Average yield per hectare is approximately 3144 kg. The crop is rainfed which only permits the production of one crop per year. Farmers producing under this system do not use standard varieties, but a mixture of varieties to minimize problems caused by inadequate management systems. Under the present system of cultivation, farmers retain about half of the crop for home consumption and seed material and sell the other half to the State-owned Rice Mill at a guaranteed price.

4.3.8.3. STRATEGIES FOR DEVELOPMENT

The strategy for the development of the local rice industry is based on the status of the local and international rice economy. The approach during the plan will be to:

(i) increase the total area under rice;

(ii) raise crop yields;

(iii) promote the vertical integration of the rice industry;

(iv) grow standardised varieties with known milling and cooling properties;

(v) purchase paddy according to standards, moisture content, etc;

(vi) promote improved cultivation practices;

(vii) produce high quality seed.

RICE REPORT 9. THE RICE SUB-SECTOR. AGRICULTURAL PLANNING DIVISION WORKING PAPER NO. 3. AUGUST, 1993 (REVISED). M. LEE & A. JACQUE. RICE INDUSTRY. CABINET DECISIONS 1981 – 1992

Table 27. Lee and Jacque rice report 1993

DATE/ cabinet minute no	DECISION(S)	COMMENTS/ STATUS
28/8/81, no 2400	agreed with effect from 1/9/81, the guaranteed price for locally produced paddy be set at $1.81/kg. or $0.89/lb.	
19/5/83, no 1409	amended (CN #2400) to reflect $1.96/kg. or $0.89/lb. with effect from 1/9/81.	
24/1/85, no 169	agreed that the price of paddy should remain at the existing level for the next 2 years (any further inducement should be through other measures for instance, subsidized ADB loans and enhancement of physical infrastructure).	

Table 27. Lee and Jacque rice report 1993 (cont.)

DATE/ cabinet minute no	DECISION(S)	COMMENTS/ STATUS
1/6/89, no 979	agreed to appoint a team to study issues relating to the production, processing and marketing of local rice and its impact on the operations on the NFM.	Team submitted report on 8/2/90.
26/4/90, no 322	-accepted report of the team and agreed that the present structure of the rice industry be maintained subject to the conditions recommended by the Minister of Food Production and Marine Exploitation, the Minister of Finance and the Minister of Industry, Enterprise and Tourism in their comments dated 23/4/90. -agreed to set up a Technical Committee to develop a grading programme and pricing structure for farmer's paddy.	Technical Committee reported in July, 1991.
7/11/91, no 2309	-Cabinet accepted the Report of the Technical Committee and agreed to: (a) implement the grading system for paddy as proposed. (b) examine the recommendation that the retail price of white rice would be increased by the Ministry of Social Development and Family Service.	Monitoring Team has been set up to oversee implementation.
25/6/92, no 1392	-agreed to price increases for locally packaged white rice and locally packaged parboiled rice. -Summary of retail price increases (a) Locally Packaged White Rice Unit Existing New Price/Packet Price 20 * $2.83 $3.31 1kg. 10* $5.49 $6.45 2kg. 4* $13.64 $16.08 5kg. 2* $26.95 $31.82 10kg.	

RICE REPORT 10. IDB BASIC AGRICULTURAL SECTOR STUDIES - RESEARCH AND TECHNOLOGY TRANSFER RICE SUB-SECTOR, MINISTRY OF FOOD PRODUCTION AND MARINE EXPLOITATION

REPORT OF AGRICULTURALIST   N. AHMAD, AUGUST 26, 1991

TAHAL CONSULTING ENGINEERS LTD.

pg. 1. Rice production in Trinidad was once much more important in the agricultural economy of the territory. For instance, in 1954, 45 percent of consumption was produced locally but this decreased to 22 percent in 1981 and by 1987, production was only 12.6 percent of consumption.

pg. 33. Development Aspects. In the physical development of the rice industry in Trinidad, three stages or approaches are identified, depending upon the size of the possible investment.

STAGE 2 pg. 33

Infrastructural improvements for the large farmers in the Plum Mitan area are envisaged. Development of rice production in this area is relatively recent and is based on completely mechanised systems of production, following technologies developed at the Caroni (1975) Rice Project. Approximately 1450 hectares of land is presently in production and there is keen interest by individual farmers to occupy lands in the area for the purpose of rice production. Basically, one crop per year is effectively grown except the largest farmer who occupies over 450 hectares of land and practices double cropping to a large extent. Substantial water resources are available in the area as several rivers drain into the greater Nariva Swamp, of which the Plum Mitan area forms a part. These natural sources would have to be supplemented by storage to enable two crops per year to be grown throughout the area.

The development of rice production in this area is presently ad hoc, unplanned and chaotic and the need for some order and regulation is most urgent, as is also the development of a policy for land acquisition and occupation. The farmers have the philosophy that increased production can be achieved by occupying increased acreages and not by intensification of production. Therefore, these valuable lands are very poorly utilised and there is much conflict among the farmers for needed resources. The great advantage in developing this area is that most of the land is state owned and the farmers are really squatters. Therefore, in theory, the area can be developed according to an approved physical plan.

STAGE 3 pg. 34

This stage envisages the comprehensive development and upgrading of the rice industry to achieve its potential in Trinidad. It would involve the development and improvement of all suitable areas for rice production including major land reclamation and infrastructural building. The large project areas would be:

(i) The Nariva Swamp   (ii) The Oropouche Lagoon   (iii) Peripheral areas of the Caroni Swamp

For the development of the first two areas, studies including project design were already carried out for the Nariva Swamp by JICA (1975) and NEDECO (1983) and for Oropouche Lagoon by SCET-AGRI (1983). pg. 35. These proposals need to be modified, if necessary, to reduce the cost of implementation and to increase their effectiveness of operation. An analysis of certain aspects of the proposals with particular emphasis on nature conservation was carried out by the University of the West Indies (1979) and useful aspects of this study should be incorporated in the planning.

RICE REPORT 11. ATTACHMENT 111 (May 1993)

POLICY ACTIONS ALREADY AGREED RE AGRICULTURAL SECTOR

CABINET MINUTE #327 DATED DECEMBER 30, 1992 MODIFIED BY ISL AGREEMENT Macro/Sectoral Policies   C. Specific subsectors

Rice Growing   Current Status   Agreed Actions

Table 28. Rice report from Cabinet minute 327 of May 1993

Policy measures in existence aim at greater self-sufficiency which has been partially achieved	Institute the transition from small plot farmers to fully mechanised farmers and/or diversification
	Improvement of agro-techniques to reduce costs
Central Rice Mill only processor of paddy	Development of irrigation schemes and infrastructure in rice growing areas
Majority of farms are less than 2 hectares	Development of research and extension programmes to improve yields and quality of paddy
High production costs	Establishment of a grading system
Total production is 18% of $13.3 m	Limit the subsidy to a level of total consumption and introduction of a grading system.
Guaranteed price exists	

RICE REPORT 12

MINISTRY OF FOOD PRODUCTION AND MARINE EXPLOITATION. FINAL REPORT 91.04.03. INTEGRATED RICE MECHANIZATION PROJECT PROPOSAL. MR. A. SEEREERAM, MR. E. LUKE, MR. J. SEALES, MR. P. RAMDEEN, MR. T. INDALSINGH. TECHNICAL ASSISTANCE PROJECT BETWEEN THE GOVERNMENT OF THE REPUBLIC OF TRINIDAD AND TOBAGO AND THE JAPANESE GOVERNMENT.

PROJECT PROFILE

1. PROJECT TITLE: INTEGRATED RICE MECHANISATION PROJECT

2. STARTING DATE: 1991

3. COMPLETION DATE: 1996; PROJECT LIFE: 5 YEARS

4. EXECUTING AGENCY: MFPME; L.W.D.D

5. PROJECT SUMMARY

This project is essentially one of research in mechanization designed to generate quantitative data in rice production for small to medium sized farms, which at present in unavailable. It will incorporate all operations from land development, planting, cultural practices, water management, harvesting and post harvesting. It will employ, among other things, existing rice technology in terms of varieties, population density, fertilization, pest/disease control, and weed control. Data generated will be analysed by multi-disciplinary teams to determine the technical and economic feasibility of various production systems and farm sizes. Such data and information will then be used to produce "tech packs" for use by Extension Officers and Subject Matter Specialists to advise rice farmers how to produce rice using modern technology to generate economic financial returns. Some primary objectives of labour cost reduction, increasing yield, improvement in quality and higher net returns, are to be evaluated.

6. PROJECT COST: (A) CAPITAL COST FOR PERIOD - $3,677,500.00

      (B)RECURRENT COST/YEAR - $200,000.00

CONTRIBUTION OF PARTIES

CAPITAL EXPENDITURE		RECURRENT COST
(A)	JICA ($TT) $3,527,500.00	
(B)	GORTT $150,000.00	$200,000.00
	$3,677,500.00	$200,000.00

References

Agristudio, 1991. Reconnaissance study for rehabilitation of the Plum Mitan rice scheme. Interim Report. Annex N4 - Climate and Hydrological Report.

Ahmad, N. 1991. IDB basic agricultural sector studies - research and technology transfer rice sub-sector, Ministry of Food Production and Marine Exploitation.

Aitken, Thomas, H.G. 1973. Bush Bush forest and the Nariva Swamp. Journal of the Trinidad Field Naturalists' Club. www.wow.net/.../Papers/BushBush/bushbush.html

Anonymous, 1999. Gender Comparative Case Study Proposal. Island Sustainability Livelihood and Equity - Gender and Development workshop, UPV, the Philippines, February, 1999.

Bacon, P.R. 1973. Appraisal of the stocks and management of sea turtles in the Caribbean and adjacent regions: Report to the Working Group on Fisheries Resources at the VIth International Coordinating Group meeting of C.I.C.A.R. in Cartagena, Columbia, July 1973.

Bacon, P. R., Kenny, J. S., Alkins, M.E., Mootoosingh, S.N., Ramcharan, E. K., and Seebaran, G.B.S. 1979. Studies on the biological resources of Nariva swamp, Trinidad. Occasional papers No. 4 of the Zoology Dept., University of the West Indies, Trinidad.

Bacon, P.R. 1988. Freshwater foodchains of Caribbean island wetlands. Acta Cientifica 2 (2-3): 74 – 93.

Bacon, Peter. 1997. Water management for sustainable development in the Nariva Swamp. In: CFCA, 1997. Nariva swamp seminar. Seminar held at Faculty of Agriculture, U.W.I., St. Augustine, Trinidad and Tobago. CFCA, Port of Spain, Trinidad

Bacon, P.R., Mahadeo, V.A. 1999. Impacts of agriculture on wetlands in Trinidad. Paper presented at Agriculture in the Caribbean: Issues and Challenges, UWI Ag.50.

Beauchamp, Tom L. 1999. The failure of theories of personhood. Kennedy Institute of Ethics Journal 9 (4). 309-324.

Boomert, A. 2006. Between the mainland and the islands: The Amerindian cultural geography of Trinidad. Paper to be presented at the symposium 'Caribbean Archaeological Research at the Peabody Museum of Natural History, Yale University: In Memory of Irving Rouse', Seventy-first Annual Meeting of the

Society for American Archaeology, San Juan, Puerto Rico, April 2006

Bonadie, Wayne A., Bacon Peter, R. 2000. Year-round utilisation of fragmented palm swamp forest by red-bellied macaws (*Ara manilata*) and orange-winged parrots (*Amazona amazonica*) in the Nariva Swamp (Trinidad). Biological Conservation 95: 1-5.

Bourdieu, P. 1977. Outline of a Theory of Practice. New York: Cambridge University Press.

Braidotti, Rosi, Ewa Charkiewicz, Sabine Hausler, Saskia Wieringa. 1994. Women, the environment, and sustainable Development: Towards a theoretical synthesis. London: Zed Books.

Brydon, Anne. 2006. The predicament of Nature: Keiko the whale and the cultural politics of whaling in Iceland. Anthropological Quarterly 79 (2): 225-260.

Castree, Noel. 1999. Contested natures. Review. Transactions of the Institute of British Geographers. New Series. 24 (4): 510 – 511.

Catton, W., Dunlap, R. 1978. Environmental Sociology: A new paradigm. The American Sociologist 13:41–9.

CFCA, 1997. Nariva swamp seminar. Seminar held at Faculty of Agriculture, U.W.I., St. Augustine, Trinidad and Tobago. CFCA, Port of Spain, Trinidad.

Clapp. R.A 2004. Wilderness ethics and political ecology: remapping the Great Bear Rainforest. Political Geography 23: 839–862.

Clayton, Susan. 2000. Models of justice in the environmental debate. Journal of Social Issues 56 (3): 459 – 474.

Conway, D. 1984. Trinidad's mismatched expectations: Planning and Development Review. Hanover, N.H.: Universities Field Staff International.

Cornwall, A. 1998. Gender, participation and the politics of difference. In: Irene Guijt and Meera Kaul Shah (eds), The Myth of Community: Gender in Participatory Development, IT Publications.

Cross, N., Dator, J., Durbal, S., Wahab, A. 1999. A pilot study of the gendered socio-cultural, socio-economic, and governance issues in the Kernahan-Cascadoux community, Nariva. Project document – Building Approaches Towards Sustainable Livelihoods. CGDS, CIDA, ISLE.

Cuevas Perez, F., Barrow, Ronald, M., and Ganpat, Roop. 1984. Trinidad and Tobago status of the rice industry. A joint paper prepared by Centre internacional de agricultura tropical (CIAT. Ministry of Agriculture, Lands and Food Production.

Central Experiment Station, Centeno, Trinidad and Tobago.

Diamond, Irene and Gloria Feman Orenstein, eds. 1990. Reweaving the World: the Emergence of Ecofeminism. San Francisco: Sierra Club Books.

Doodhai, M. 2000. A simple life. Kernaham is one of South's hidden treasures. Sunday Guardian June 4, 2000. pg 8.

Dove, M.R., and Kammen, D.M. 1997. The epistemology of sustainable resource use: managing forest products, swiddens, and high-yielding variety crops. Human Organisation 56 (1): 91 - 101.

Draft estimate 1984 recurrent expenditure rice maintenance programme, 1983. Agricultural engineering and development division, Ministry of Agriculture, Lands and Food Production, Trinidad.

Draft National Policy for Food and Agriculture, 1993. Republic of Trinidad and Tobago.

Draft Second Five - Year Plan 1964 - 1968. National Planning Commission: Dr. Eric Williams, Mr. Arthur, N. Robinson, Mr. John O'Halloran, Mr. Robert Wallace, Mr. Lionel Robinson, Mr. Louis Alan Reece, Mr. Jack Harewood, Mrs. Patricia Robinson, Mr. David Weintraub, Mr. William Demas. Government Printery, Trinidad and Tobago, 1963. Chapter XIV pgs. 173, 179, 201..203

Duguid, A., Downie, R., Heath, M., Hambly, C. 1996. A comparison between fish communities in Nariva Swamp and adjacent rice paddies. Report of the University of Glasgow Exploration Society, pp – 22 – 27.

Driver, T. Watershed management, land tenure and forests in the Northern Range, Trinidad. In: Leach Melissa, Amanor Kojo and Fairhead James. 2001. Forest science and forest policy: Knowledge, instituions and policy processes. Final Report to ESCOR of the Department for International Development (DFID), Project No. R7211 http://www.ids.ac.uk/ids/KNOTS/PDFs/ForestESCORReport.pdf.

Dunlap, Riley E., Catton, William Jr. 1979. Environmental sociology. Annual Review of Sociology 5: 243-73.

Durbal, Sharda. 2000. Natural resource use and management in Kernahan and Cascadoux. Nariva Swamp: A gendered case study: Social, cultural and gendered analysis of Kernahan and Cascadoux. The Centre for Gender and Development Studies, The University of the West Indies, St. Augustine.

Elam, Mark. 1999. Living dangerously with Bruno Latour in a hybrid world. Theory, Culture and Society 16: 1 - 24.

FAO, 1957. Report to the government of Trinidad and Tobago on the reclamation of the Caroni, Oropouche and Nariva areas. Report No. 636. Food and Agriculture Organisation, Rome. 111 pp.

Forestry Division, 1987. Annual report of the Forestry Division for the year 1987. Trinidad and Tobago.

Foucault, Michel. 1980. Power/Knowledge: Selected Interviews and Other Writings, 1972–1977, ed. Colin Gordon. New York: Pantheon.

Gaard, Greta. 1998. Ecological Politics: Ecofeminists and the Greens. Philadelphia: Temple University Press.

Gerber, Lisa. 2002. Standing Humbly Before Nature. Ethics & the Environment 7 (1): 39-53.

Ghany, H. 1996. (Editor). Kamal: a lifetime of politics, religion and culture. Dr. Kamaluddin Mohammed Publisher, San Juan.

Hardjoeno, Vanderzwaag, D., Shaw, T., Bedeno, J.A.S., Sirju-Charran, G. 1996. Governance. Position paper. Workshop on core-course of Island Sustainability, Livelihood and Equity. Ujung Padang, 1 - 6 December 1996. Indonesia.

Hettinger, Ned. 2002. The problem of finding a positive role for humans in the natural world. Ethics & the Environment. 7(1):109-123.

Hosein, G., Cross, Nicole. 2000. Nariva Swamp: A gendered case study: Social, cultural and gendered analysis of Kernahan and Cascadoux. The Centre for Gender and Development Studies, UWI, St. Augustine.

Huggan, Graham. 2004. "Greening" Postcolonialism: Ecocritical Perspectives. MFS Modern Fiction Studies 50(3): 701-733.

Institute of Marine Affairs, 1998. Final Report for the Environmental Impact Assessment of the Nariva Swamp (Biche Bois Neuf Area). IMA/MALMR, Trinidad and Tobago.

Institute of Marine Affairs, 1999. Final Report: Formulation of the Nariva Swamp Management Plan. IMA/MALMR, Trinidad and Tobago.

Jackson, C. 1993. Environmentalisms and gender interests in the Third World. Development and Change 24: 649 - 677.

Jacques, Peter. 2006. The rearguard of modernity: Environmental skepticism as a struggle of citizenship. Global Environmental Politics 6:76 – 101.

James, K. 1994. The Potential of Bush bush wildlife sanctuary, Trinidad for ecotourism. Undergraduate thesis, B.Sc., Zoology/Chemistry. UWI. 97 pp.

Joekes, S., Heyzer, N., Oniang'o, R, Salles, Y. 1994. Gender, environment and population. Development and Change 25: 137 - 165.

Kacal, S., Homer, F. 1993. Recommendations for 3 National Parks; Matura, Nariva and North East Tobago, unpublished.

Kacal, S. 1997. Nariva issues: looking toward community co-management. In: Nariva swamp seminar. Seminar held at Faculty of Agriculture, U.W.I., St. Augustine, Trinidad and Tobago. CFCA, Port of Spain, Trinidad (pg 60.)

Kacal, S. 2000. Social assessment and community action plan of Nariva managed resource are. Final report prepared for Ministry of Agriculture, Land and Marine Resources, GORTT and World Bank. Unpublished.

Kalema-Zikusoka, Gladys. 2005. Protected areas, human livelihoods and healthy animals: Ideas for improvements in conservation and development interventions. In: Osofsky, Steven A., Cleaveland, Sarah, Karesh, William B., Kock, Michael D., Nyhus, Philip J., Starr, Lisa, Yang, Angela, (eds.). Conservation and Development Interventions at the Wildlife/Livestock Interface. The World Conservation Union (IUCN).

Keeler, A.G.and Pemberton, C. 1996. Nariva swamp: an exercise in environmental economics. Notes from a seminar presented at the University of the West Indies, St. Augustine, Nov. 20, 1996.

Kupfer, J.H. 2003. Engaging Nature aesthetically. Journal of Aesthetic Education 37 (1): 77 – 89.

Lans, C. 1996. The price of rice. Express. Monday July 15, 1996. pp. 15.

Leach, Melissa, Fairhead James. 2001. Science, policy and national parks in Trinidad and Tobago. Working Paper from the project 'Forest Science and Forest Policy: Knowledge, Institutions and Policy Processes'. Also presented at the Workshop 'Changing perspectives on forests: ecology, people and science/policy processes in West Africa and the Caribbean', 26-27 March 2001 at The Institute of Development Studies, University of Sussex.

Lee, M. and Jacque, A. 1993. The rice sub-sector. Agricultural planning division working paper no. 3. (revised).

Leftwich, A. 1994. Governance, the State and the Politics of Development. Development and Change 25:363 - 386.

Locke, C. 1999. Constructing a gender policy for joint forest management in India.

Development and Change 30: 265 - 285.

MacGregor, Sherilyn. 2004. From care to citizenship: Calling ecofeminism back to politics. Ethics & the Environment 9 (1):56-84.

Mack-Canty, Colleen. 2004. Third-Wave Feminism and the Need to Reweave the Nature/Culture Duality NWSA Journal 16 (3): 154-179.

MacMillan, A. 1967. Aranjuez: Agricultural Development in a suburban setting. University of the West Indies, St. Augustine, Trinidad.

Maharaj, K. 2000. A simple life. Sunday Express Section 2, May 14 2000 pg 31.

Mahy, M. 1997. Feasibility of co-managing a wetland of international importance: the case of the Nariva Swamp, Trinidad. Unpublished thesis. Master of Environmental Studies, Dalhousie University, Halifax, Nova Scotia, Canada.

MALMR, date unknown. Review of agricultural trade and pricing policy. Final report. Prepared for the Ministry of Agriculture, Land and Marine Resources on behalf of the IDB by Carlisle A. Pemberton.

MALMR, 1983. A draft national policy for food and agriculture. Republic of Trinidad and Tobago. May 1993. Attachment 1.

MALMR, 1995. Review of the agriculture sector 1993. Prepared by the agricultural planning division, Ministry of Agriculture, Land and Marine Resources. Jan 1995.

McCauley, D.J. 2006. Selling out on nature. Nature 443 (7107): 27-8.

Merchant, Carolyn. 1980. The death of nature: Women, ecology, and the scientific revolution. San Francisco: Harper and Row.

Mies, Maria, Shiva Vandana. 1993. Ecofeminism. London: Zed Books.

Mies, Maria. 1986. Patriarchy and accumulation on a world scale: Women in the international division of labor. Atlantic Highlands, NJ: Zed Books.

Miller, Daniel. 1994. Modernity, An Ethnographic Approach: Dualism and Mass Consumption in Trinidad , Oxford and Providence: Berg.

Ministry of Agriculture, Lands and Marine Resources, 1994. Draft. White Paper. Food and Agriculture Policy.

Mohammed, Patricia. 1995. Writing Gender into History: the negotiation of gender relations among Indian men and women in post-indenture Trinidad society, 1914 - 47. In V. Shepherd, Bridget Brereton & Barbara Bailey (Eds.), Engendering History: Caribbean women in historical perspective . Jamaica: Ian Randle

Publishers.

Mootoosingh, S.N., 1979. The growth of conservation awareness in Trinidad and Tobago (1965-1979). Occasional paper no.3, Dept. of Zoology, UWI (St. Augustine).

Mosse, D. 1997. The symbolic making of a commmon property resource: history, ecology and locality in a tank-irrigated landscape in South India. Development and Change 28: 467 - 504.

Murdoch, J. 2001. Ecologising sociology: Actor-Network Theory, co-construction and the problem of human exemptionalism. Sociology, 35(1): 111-133.

Murphy, Raymond. 1995. Sociology as if Nature did not matter: An ecological critique. The British Journal of Sociology 46 (4): 688 – 707.

Murray, T., Benn, A., Cross, N., de Souza, G., Manwaring, G., Siung Chnag, A., Stewart-Henry, A., Sturm, M. 1992. Report of the Task Force appointed to make recommendations on specific issues for the development of a national policy on aquaculture in Trinidad and Tobago.

Nathai-Gyan, Nadra. 1997. Conservation status of the Nariva wetland. In: CFCA, 1997. Nariva swamp seminar. Seminar held at Faculty of Agriculture, U.W.I., St. Augustine, Trinidad and Tobago. CFCA, Port of Spain, Trinidad.

National Policy on Wetland Conservation. Trinidad and Tobago. Draft prepared by the National Wetland Committee. January 16, 1996.

NEDECO, 1981. A summary and review of previous studies of the Nariva Swamp. Technical Note No. 4. Netherlands Engineering Consultants. 40 pp.

NEDECO, 1983. Phase 1 - Investigations on the development of the Nariva Swamp. Vol. 1. Main Report. Final Report. Ministry of Agriculture, Lands and Fisheries, Port of Spain. 36 pp.

OCTA, 1970. Nariva Swamp Development Project. Feasibility Report. Overseas Technical Co-operation Agency of Japan. 212 pp.

Operational review of the Trinidad and Tobago rice mill complex. Draft working document. Data collection, analysis and recommendations. April 1981. FAC. Planning Associates Ltd., POS.

Paul, F. 1998. Farmers call for IMA report on Nariva Swamp. Trinidad Guardian Friday October 16, 1998 pg 5.

Ramsar Convention, 1995. Monitoring Procedure, Nariva Swamp, Trinidad and

Tobago. Gland, Switzerland.

Ramsar Convention, 1996. Final Report, Monitoring Procedure, Nariva Swamp, Trinidad and Tobago. Ramsar Convention. Gland, Switzerland.

Ramsar, 1996. Final Report, Monitoring Procedure, Nariva Swamp, Trinidad and Tobago. Ramsar Convention. Gland, Switzerland.

Review of the Agriculture sector (1993), 1995. Prepared by the Agricultural Planning Division, Ministry of Agriculture, Land and Marine Resources. T&T.

Rocheleau, D., Thomas-Slayter, B., Wangari, E. 1996. Gender and environment: a feminist political ecology perspective. In: Rocheleau, D., Thomas-Slayter, B., Wangari, E. 1996 (eds.). Feminist political ecology: global issues and local experiences. Routledge, London and New York. Pp. 1-23.

Rostant, R. 1998. Nariva comes back from the brink – Rice farmers want to be allowed back. Trinidad Guardian February 2, 1998.

Rowley, M. 1996?. Gender and the environment: a Caribbean perspective. paper presented at the workshop on Gender and Island Sustainability, UWI, St. Augustine, Jan. 13 - 17, 1997.

Seereeram, A., Luke, E., Seales, J., Ramdeen, P., Indalsingh, T. 1991. Final report 91.04.03. Integrated rice mechanisation project proposal. Technical assistance project between the Government of the Republic of Trinidad and Tobago and the Japanese Government. Ministry of Food Production and Marine Exploitation.

Shiva, Vandana. 1989. Staying Alive: Women, Ecology and Development. Delhi/London: Zed Books.

Siurua, Hanna. 2006. Nature above people: Rolston and "Fortress" conservation in the South. Ethics & the Environment 11 (1):71-96.

Sletto Bjørn. 2002. Producing space(s), representing landscapes: Maps and resource conflicts in Trinidad. Cultural Geographies 9: 389–420.

Steer, H.J. and Benson, E.G. 1953. A survey of the rice industry. Statistical studies and papers no. 2. Rice division of the Department of Agriculture and the CSO.

Stone, Christopher, D. 1974. Should trees have legal standing? Toward legal rights for natural objects. California: William Kaufman, Inc.

Sutton, P.K. 1981. Forged from the love of liberty. Selected speeches of Dr. Eric Williams. Compilation. Longman Caribbean.

Taitt, G. 1999. Rice, culture and government in Trinidad 1897 – 1939. In Colonial

Caribbean in Transition: Essays on Postemancipation Social and Cultural History. Edited by Bridget Brereton and Kelvin A. Yelvington. Gainesville: University Press of Florida; Kingston: The Press, UWI.

Thelen, K.D. and Faizool, S. 1980. Plan for a system of national parks and other protected areas in Trinidad and Tobago. Forestry Division, Ministry of Agriculture Lands and Fisheries, POS, Trinidad. 106 pp.

Tompkins, E., Adger, W .Neil. 2002. Institutional networks for inclusive coastal management in Trinidad and Tobago. Environment and Planning A. 34:1095 – 1111.

UNDP, 2000. Gender in development. Gender Analysis: Alternative paradigms. Http://www.undp.org/gender/resources/mono6a.html.

Utting, P. 1994. Social and political dimensions of environmental protection in Central America. Development and Change 25: 231 - 259.

Wahab, A. 1997. The status of women in the Nariva wetland communities: A case study. Unpublished.

Wahab, A.S. 1997. Stakeholders' perceptions of natural resource conflict - the case of the Nariva wetland, Trinidad and Tobago. Unpublished M.Sc. Thesis, Shimane University, Japan.

Warren, K.J. and J. Cheney, 1991. Ecological feminism and ecosystem ecology. Hypatia 6 (1): 244 - 262.

White paper on Agriculture, 1979. Ministry of Agriculture, Lands and Fisheries. Government printery, Trinidad and Tobago.

Wildlife Section, 1993. Historical perspectives on habitat destruction in the Nariva Swamp, Trinidad: A Wildlife Section Issues Paper. Wildlife Section, Forestry Division, Ministry of Agriculture, Land and Marine Resources, St. Joseph, Trinidad and Tobago.

Willems-Braun, Bruce. 1997. Buried epistemologies: The politics of Nature in (post) colonial British Columbia. Annals of the Association of American Geographers. 87 (1): 3-31.

Wolfe, Cary. 2003. Old orders for new: Ecology, animal rights, and the poverty of humanism. In: Animal Rites: American Culture, the Discourse of Species, and Posthumanist Theory. Chicago: U of Chicago. Pp. 21-43.

Worth, C. Brooke. 1967. A naturalist in Trinidad. Philadelphia and New York: J.B. Lippincott.

Index

www.ingramcontent.com/pod-product-compliance
Lightning Source LLC
Chambersburg PA
CBHW081655270326
41933CB00017B/3179